I'm Dreaming
of a Green Christmas

GIFTS, DECORATIONS, AND RECIPES THAT
USE LESS AND MEAN MORE

by ANNA GETTY

photographs by RON HAMAD

CHRONICLE BOOKS

SAN FRANCISCO

Copyright © 2009 by Anna Getty.

Photographs copyright © 2009 by Ron Hamad.

Library of Congress Cataloging-in-Publication Data:

Getty, Anna.

 I'm dreaming of a green Christmas : gifts, decorations, and recipes that use less and mean more / by Anna Getty.

 p. cm.

 Includes index.

 ISBN: 978-0-8118-6767-2

 1. Christmas decorations. 2. Handicraft. 3. Cookery. 4. Sustainable living. I. Title.

 TT900.C4G354 2009

 745.594'12—dc22

2008035028

Manufactured in China

Designed by Anne Donnard

The photographs in this book were made possible by the generous contribution of sustainable waves from Kelly Green Design + Home in Los Angeles.

10 9 8 7 6 5 4 3 2 1

Chronicle Books LLC
680 Second Street
San Francisco, California 94107
www.chroniclebooks.com

I'm Dreaming
of a Green Christmas

this book is dedicated to a
healthy and thriving planet

contents

foreword

AH, THE HOLIDAYS. A time of family, tradition, and of course, shopping. In America we clearly love the shopping part, racking up half our annual purchases between Thanksgiving and early January. When I heard my friend and trusted eco-confidante Anna Getty was authoring a book on greening up this notoriously superficial season, I knew we were about to be given invaluable insight into what the holidays really mean. Amid a sea of consumption, we need Anna's thoughtful perspectives on celebrating a green Christmas.

As the founder of Ecofabulous.com, a web site devoted to "sustainable, sexy style" and the "green guru" for various magazines, television shows, and radio spots, I make it my mission in life to show people how fabulous living green can be. It is truly exciting to discover that everything associated with the holidays can have a more sustainable, but equally fulfilling, alternative. I love how this book gives us practical, tangible ways to increase the pleasure of the holidays while decreasing our environmental impact. Rethinking our purchases and our actions this season is simply "eco-wise."

Over the last seven years, my family has been decorating a fun reclaimed plastic tree with the same ornaments, which are imbued with more sentimental value each year they hang from our glimmering faux branches. On family trips we'll sometimes bring something sustainable back to remember our sojourn. Eventually it gets strung on our "tree." We're a mixed-religion family and appreciate the joyful custom of dressing something up together. For families who view that real tree in the house as simply a must, I always recommend buying a potted one that can be planted after the holidays. There are even organizations that will drop off, pick up, and plant a tree for you—now *that's* a holiday gift (see Resources).

I've spent holidays past with Anna and her eclectic but very close family. I admire how she embraces ritual and tradition in her celebrations, which *always* are mindful of the environment. For instance, one Easter she hid free-range eggs (that were colored with nontoxic dyes) and surprised our daughters with organic chocolate bunnies and FSC-certified wooden toys. The kids noticed only how generous the Easter bunny had been that year, but I certainly appreciated how mindful our celebration was.

Anna and I are constant collaborators. Currently we're working on her eco retreat in Italy, which will be a stellar example of gorgeous sustainability. We're both on the board of Healthy Child, Healthy World, an organization that educates the public about toxins, and we mutually support our other environmental charity commitments, such as Global Green, Mikhail Gorbachev's not-for-profit organization focused on sustainable and equitable building solutions. The boundless love Anna exhibits toward her daughter, her passionate devotion to the earth, and her inherent sense of all things chic make her well suited to shed light on how easy and elegant it is to make the earth one of our holiday priorities. This book not only provides tips and instructions for creating green Christmas traditions, but also encourages us to reassess where we place importance during the holidays—or any celebration, for that matter. From the cards to the wrapping paper to the gifts to the food to the decorations, everything about the holidays can be reinvigorated and celebrated in a more sustainable way. Take gifts; it's not very thoughtful to give someone a petroleum-based candle that's going to emit toxins into the air, or pajamas that have been treated with chemical fire retardants. Soy-based candles, organic-cotton PJs, or handmade gifts say that you truly care about the recipient. And by choosing to serve your loved ones organic fare, you can make your family festivities take on an even more meaningful tone.

Anna is one of the most creative, committed, and kind women I have ever known. In this book, she offers us a fresh new way to look at the holidays. Her outlook takes the focus off thoughtless consumption and shines a light on family, time-honored traditions, and the environment. She doesn't ask us to ban purchases, but rather encourages us to buy consciously and think about what Christmas really means to us. This is a guide to help all of us discover old and new ways to celebrate abundance. Namaste.

ZEM JOAQUIN
Founder and Editor-in-Chief, Ecofabulous

introduction

When I was young, the holidays were very simple and all about tradition, family, and being together. Spending the holiday with my mom and grandparents in Germany, I cherished the simplicity of walks on snowy evenings, carrying lanterns with candles burning bright. I loved spending Christmas with my mom, who focused on bringing nature inside. My mom's goal was to make the holiday as magical as possible for my brother and me. She always decorated the tree on Christmas Eve, a German tradition that leaves tree-trimming to the adults for the children to discover. Then we would wait in our bedrooms and emerge a bit later to a festive holiday scene with walnuts and fresh cranberries.

During holidays back in the States, we hiked through the redwood forest in Marin County, north of San Francisco, and collected moss, twigs, and rocks that we used to create magical little kingdoms in shoe boxes. We watched the *Nutcracker* ballet, mesmerized by the dancers, and sipped mugs of hot chocolate made with soy milk and Indian spices.

Of course our holidays, like every family's, came with their fair share of drama. One year our house caught fire. We returned from a ski trip to find that half the house had burned down. It was my family's first experience with losing something so significant; the furniture was burned, and the house was a mess. But it allowed us to focus on gratitude (no one had been hurt) and appreciate the nonmaterial gifts in our lives. While losing our house was a shock, I'll never forget the closeness I felt that Christmas, with my family safe and sound around me.

These experiences and memories inspired me to return to my green roots about five years ago, when I started spending more time working with organic food organizations and other environmental nonprofits, educating myself about healthful eating and healthy living. When I realized that Christmas was moving away from the wonderful simplicity of my youth, I decided to turn my knowledge toward making my family's holiday celebrations more sustainable.

It's amazing how the simple things also happen to be the most environmentally sound choices, such as choosing to spend time with family, cooking, baking, talking, or making decorations instead of driving to a mall and spending hours shopping. As a child I attended a Waldorf school, whose philosophy is very much about a connection to nature and the earth and the magic of that connection. My family made simple ornaments from chestnuts, walnuts, and other edible items and from salt, flour, and water. These simple craft ideas create beautiful decorations as well as lasting memories. Through my mom I have a definite connection with nature, and that's the first step toward creating truly sustainable holiday traditions. The more you can do outside during the holidays, the better—taking walks in the snow or on the beach, renting a cabin, or hiking in a national forest and breathing that fresh winter air. Establish a connection to nature, your family, and your community. Even though my family wasn't religious, we always attended Christmas Eve mass and loved celebrating with the community, shaking hands with our neighbors and embracing our friends.

The Christmas season arrives amid a flurry of activity: planning holiday parties, trimming the tree, stringing lights, selecting and wrapping gifts, and cooking meals for guests. Sometimes those purchases and plans steal the spotlight from the joy and traditions that mark this festive time of year. In all that seasonal frenzy and merrymaking, it's easy to forget the unintended consequences our celebrations have on the planet. During the holidays, household waste increases by more than 25 percent. In fact, according to the Ecology Center in Berkeley, California, Americans throw away an additional five million tons of trash between Thanksgiving and New Year's Eve.

I wrote this book with those scary statistics in mind, but also with the idea that an earth-friendly holiday doesn't need to detract from the traditional joys of Christmas. In fact, giving back to the planet doesn't mean cutting back, and I am not advocating that you start over by throwing things out and buying green. Rather, look around and reuse what's already in your house. You might be surprised by what you can recycle: a handful of wine corks transforms into a festive collection of name-card holders; an old cashmere sweater takes on new life as a pillow; a stack of old Christmas cards becomes a wealth of cheerful gift tags. My decorating ideas and sumptuous recipes will keep your holiday traditions alive in an eco-friendly manner. I offer green inspiration to help you choose unique gifts (including delicious edible ones), make simple yet stunning decorations for every room in your house, and prepare mouthwatering meals featuring organic ingredients.

Indeed, a great path to a greener holiday runs right through your kitchen. I was raised in an organic-

vegetarian household, and for the holidays my mother filled the table with delectable seasonal dishes. I've used her simplicity as my inspiration in this book's recipes. I encourage you to buy only organic, seasonal, and local ingredients for your holiday feasts, and I created the recipes in this book with those goals in mind.

For many parents, including me, making environmentally friendly decisions is particularly important, because we want to show our children what the holidays really represent: sharing, gratitude, and tradition. Such ideals are particularly relevant in this day and age, when life moves so fast and can be so stressful. And you just may discover that by slowing down and eliminating a lot of the usual clutter from your celebration, you not only will be honoring the planet and creating bright new holiday traditions with your family, you also will be more relaxed. I certainly did.

If you want to create memorable Christmas traditions while taking small steps to reduce your carbon footprint, minimize waste, and creatively reuse what you already have, this book is for you. Many people see going green as a challenge, but when I read David Wann's book *Simple Prosperity: Finding Real Wealth in a Sustainable Lifestyle*, I realized that it's a celebratory one—and that it doesn't have to be difficult. By consuming less, we enrich our lives and our community. Challenge yourself and your family to produce less waste this holiday season. The ideas in this book, and the Resources list at the end, will give you a start. And you might just find that these ideas and tips will help you stay green all year long—an excellent New Year's resolution.

THE TEN EASIEST THINGS
YOU CAN DO *to* SAVE ENERGY DURING THE HOLIDAYS

1. SWITCH YOUR TWINKLY LIGHTS TO LED LIGHTS. Energy use skyrockets around the holidays. A 2003 study conducted by the U.S. Department of Energy determined that Americans consume about 2,220 GWh (gigawatt hours) of electricity each holiday season by using standard incandescent holiday lights. The study found that a 20 percent shift by American households to LED lights would save 440 GWh of electricity during the estimated thirty-day holiday season.

2. LOWER YOUR THERMOSTAT. If there's a fire burning in the fireplace, lower the thermostat to conserve energy (and save on your heating bill). You definitely can lower the temperature if you're throwing a party—the body heat will more than make up for it. As a matter of fact, try to keep your thermostat at 68 degrees Fahrenheit (20 degrees Celsius) throughout the winter; you will see a huge difference in your energy bill.

3. INSULATE YOUR HOME. Heating and cooling account for 44 percent of household energy use, and proper insulation slows the rate at which heat escapes in the winter. Be sure to plug up any leaks or cracks in your house, and if possible, replace windows with energy-efficient models.

4. TURN DOWN THE TEMPERATURE OF YOUR WATER HEATER. Keep your water heater at the warm (120 degrees Fahrenheit/50 degrees Celsius) setting and insulate the water pipes to decrease heat loss between uses.

5. TURN OFF THE LIGHTS when you're not home and while you're asleep, and that means your Christmas tree lights and any outdoor holiday lights too. Ideally, lights should be on for no more than six hours a day. Use mirrors to double the amount of light while the lights are on.

6. PLAN YOUR SHOPPING TRIPS CAREFULLY. Make one trip to the mall instead of three, which will save gas. Walking to stores or carpooling with friends is even better. Another way to reduce fuel consumption is to buy locally; shopping in your hometown supports the local merchants and strengthens the community, and it cuts fuel use if you walk to town.

7. BURN BETTER WOOD. Cozying up to a crackling fire? Save a tree and burn some all-natural man-made logs instead. Java-Logs are the greenest option; made entirely from coffee grounds, they are 100 percent natural, and their ashes are compostable. See the Resources section for information about these and other types of logs. These planet-friendly fireplace choices will keep you warm all night long. And when you're not using the fireplace, close the flue and block the fireplace to prevent heat from escaping. (For more on fireplaces, see page 30.)

8. AVOID JUNK MAIL. While Christmas shopping online or in stores, be sure not to get on the catalog mailing lists. Junk mail annually accounts for fifty-three million trees and enough water to fill eighty-one thousand Olympic-size pools. Go to www.catalogchoice.org or www.directmail.com to get off the lists.

9. BUY LOCALLY. Buying food and goods locally is the best way to reduce energy use.

10. DISPOSE OF YOUR WASTE PROPERLY. Disposing of waste properly ensures that less energy is used for unnecessary waste build up in landfills, recycling plants, and other waste collection centers. Help your community save energy by creating less waste and making sure it goes to the most resourceful locations. For more on recycling, see page 161.

nesting

Our **homes**, which center us throughout the year, become even more important around the holidays. Make it a priority to create an inviting, welcoming space in which you can relax and enjoy the season with your family and friends. But making your home look festive is not the only **fun** and vital ingredient to **Christmas preparations**. Planning meals, gatherings, and celebrations in your own home is also key, and it allows you to draw on your existing resources, such as **decorations**, linens, dishware, flatware, and glassware. Focusing on the home means spending time with friends and family, and with school holidays, kids have more time to be involved. I love to cook with my daughter, and I also love setting up **crafts** for her and her friends. Family dinners are the most important part of my holiday celebrations, so I've included some of my favorite recipes that incorporate the bounty of the season.

Both indoors and out, small changes to your Christmas preparations will add up to lots of planet-friendly decorations. Hanging a **handmade** wreath on the door is a sign of welcome, and that's the first thing I do. While you're decorating, remember to reuse what you've bought for previous holidays and think about how you can wrap it and store it for next year. (You'll find more on that in the Reflecting chapter.)

nature garland

This lovely nature-inspired garland is perfect to hang around a doorway, on a banister, on the wall, or draped across a mantel. By choosing objects you already have around the house, you can incorporate your own meaningful memorabilia into the holiday season and avoid acquiring more clutter. This is also a great way to incorporate beautiful nature pieces from the outdoors in your decorations.

GATHER

CREATE

- 1 piece of ribbon about 6 feet long/183 cm (the exact length depends on where you will hang the garland)

- Small lengths of used ribbon or raffia to hang items (5 to 7 inches/13 to 18 cm each)

- Feathers, mistletoe, old Christmas cards, family photographs, cinnamon sticks, pinecones, berry branches (juniper works well and is in season), small bells, and any other Christmas-themed items you like. (Just make sure the decorative items don't weigh too much. Use lightweight, dainty objects; heavier ones will weigh the garland down.)

- Tape

- Nontoxic glue

1. Decide where you would like to display the garland and measure the length of the space. Cut a piece of used gift ribbon or raffia accordingly.

2. Cut one 5- to 7-inch/13- to 18-cm length of ribbon for each decorative object you're using. Tie, tape, or glue the ribbon to each individual item, creating a loop that you will string onto the long piece of ribbon. (Tie the ribbon to the berry branches and feathers, but use tape or glue for the photographs and cards.)

3. String the items onto the long ribbon, spacing them 2 to 3 inches/5 to 8 cm apart, depending on how many you've chosen. Hang the garland with thumbtacks or any existing hooks, or use a hammer and nails.

| MORE GARLANDS |

Bay leaves: Bay leaves are in season in winter. Look for fresh organic bay leaves. Once it has dried, you can use the garland for years to come. Use recycled ribbon or light-gauge florist wire to connect the branches together.

Vintage toys: Tie vintage Christmas-themed toys and stuffed animals together with red ribbon and lay the garland on top of your mantel.

Pine branches: This is a classic. Ask your local florist or Christmas tree vendor for broken pine branches and make a pine garland. It will make your house smell so good. Use light-gauge florist wire to connect the branches together. After Christmas, add the garland to your yard waste bin; it will be turned into mulch. Be sure to remove florist wire before discarding branches.

pinecone and nut wreath

To me, a pinecone and nut wreath is a gift direct from nature. It looks just as beautiful on an outside door as it does hanging in the house or in the garden. In the dining room, place these wreaths on the table with candelabras in the center for a striking visual effect.

GATHER

- Pinecones of varying sizes and shapes (you will use anywhere from 25 to 100 pinecones, depending on the size of the wreath)
- Old towel
- Baking sheets
- Used aluminum foil
- 1 roll of light-gauge florist wire
- Wire cutters
- Wire wreath frame (For best results, use a size 2 or 3 wire base; see Resources for suppliers. You also can use a wire hanger, but the wreath will not look as full.)
- 20 to 30 nuts in their shell, such as walnuts, hazelnuts, almonds, and chestnuts
- Nontoxic glue gun
- Gloves (garden or rubber) (optional; if the pinecones are prickly, gloves make handling easier)
- 24-inch/61-cm piece of used ribbon or raffia (optional)

CREATE

1. Preheat the oven to 200°F/90°C.

2. Wash the pinecones. Fill the kitchen sink or bathtub with 2 to 3 inches/5 to 8 cm of lukewarm water. Place the pinecones in the water and swoosh them around to remove any dirt or bugs. Drain the water, rinse the pinecones, and dry them with an old towel.

3. Line the baking sheets with the used aluminum foil, arrange the pinecones on the sheets, and bake for 30 minutes. (Baking the pinecones dries them out, removes the resin—and makes your home smell extra Christmasy!) Note: wash and bake the pinecones only if you're using pinecones you collected outside. Skip this step for pinecones purchased at a florist shop. Be sure to ask the florist if they have been cleaned.

4. Cut as many 7- to 8-inch /17- to 20-cm pieces of light-gauge florist wire as you have pinecones. Fold the wire pieces in half.

5. Wrap a folded wire piece around the first pinecone and twist the loose ends tight around the pinecone to make sure the wire is secure. Repeat with the remaining wire pieces and pinecones.

6. Starting with the larger pinecones, and working from the inside of the wreath frame out and the bottom to the top, attach each pinecone's wire securely to the bottom wire of the wreath frame. Wire the second pinecone snugly next to the first, and repeat with each successive cone, keeping the pinecones snug against one another.

7. Once the wreath is as full as you want it, take the nuts and glue them to the pinecones. Make sure you find secure grooves in the wreath where you can easily attach the nuts.

NOTE: *Wreath frames are available in any craft store around the holidays (see Resources). Prewashed pinecones are available at your local florist.*

| OPTIONAL |

Take the ribbon or raffia and make a bow. Cut one 6-inch/15-cm piece of florist wire and loop it through the back of the bow. Twist the loop of florist wire around a pinecone near the top of the wreath. Cut the ends of the bow to the desired length.

| TAKING DECORATIONS OUTSIDE |

Decorating the exterior of your house doesn't require yards of holiday lights. Take a break from the light switch and create a holiday glow with other types of decorations.

- Display vintage decorations, such as tin Santas or ceramic deer from flea markets or garage sales.

- Make deer and Christmas trees out of wire, or look for decorative reindeer made from willow twigs; many eco-conscious retailers sell them (see Resources).

- Cut snowflakes from recycled paper, cardboard, or fabric scraps and hang them in your windows.

- Create decorative arrangements of ornaments or other pretty objects on your windowsills and set a soy candle next to each to illuminate it (for more on candles, see page 68). If you have decorations that require holiday lights, switch to LED lights (for more on these, see page 32).

| HITTING THE ROAD |

Many of us have to travel over the holidays to visit family and friends. Travel, of course, wreaks havoc on the planet, primarily through the burning of fossil fuels, which contributes to global warming and creates air, noise, and water pollution. Here are a few things you can do to offset the environmental damage.

- Compensate for your travel-related carbon footprint through a company like TerraPass, which offsets your resource use by funding clean-energy projects. (See www.terrapass.com for more information.)

- If possible, take a bus or a train; these are the least-polluting modes of long-distance transportation. If you're driving to grandma's house, try to carpool with other family members to reduce the number of cars on the road. Driving is often a better choice than flying; for many short to medium flights, airplanes emit more heat-trapping gases per person than cars do. (The International Ecotourism Society estimates that 10 percent of all greenhouse gases come from air travel.) If you must fly, try to get a direct flight; the most fuel is burned during takeoffs and landings.

- Pack lighter: Instead of bringing gifts, which weigh down suitcases and consequently require more fuel to be burned in both airplanes and cars, try to do your shopping locally. This also eliminates the need to ship the gifts, which is extremely unfriendly to the planet. (For more on green shipping, see page 121.)

- Stay at a green hotel. Most hotels now give guests the option of having their linens and towels changed every other day, rather than every day, which saves water and natural resources. And bring your own toiletries instead of using the individually packaged items provided by the hotel.

- If you're visiting a new city, try to walk as much as possible instead of taking taxis or tour buses. If you have to rent a car, choose the most fuel-efficient model possible (preferably a hybrid). Most car rental companies have a "green fleet" to choose from.

- Don't forget to turn off the lights and unplug appliances before you leave for your trip.

EXPERT GREEN TIP

JOSH DORFMAN, *founder and CEO, Vivavi, and author of*
The Lazy Environmentalist: Your Guide to Easy, Stylish Green Living

www.lazyenvironmentalist.com

When heading home for the holidays, join a ride-share service and give a ride to somebody else going your way. Sites like Zimride.com make ride-sharing easy and fun by allowing you to create and view personal profiles before choosing to ride together. The more we ride-share, the more we reduce greenhouse gas emissions by taking cars off the road. By sharing your ride, you give a gift to another person and to the planet.

recycled wool wreath

Every couple of years I give away a bag of sweaters to Goodwill. This playful Christmas wreath is another good use of your old sweaters, especially the ones with holes, which Goodwill probably would not accept.

GATHER

CREATE

- Scissors
- Old sweaters in different colors and textures from friends and family
- Wire hanger
- Wire cutters
- Needle and thread

1. With the scissors, cut the sweaters into 2-by-2-inch/5-by-5-cm squares. You probably will need 250 to 300 squares for one 13-inch/33-cm wreath, depending on the thickness of the sweaters. Keep one arm of a sweater intact for the last step. This may take time, so turn on some tunes and open a good bottle of organic wine while you cut the squares.

2. Untwist the ends of the wire hanger and reshape it into a circle. Push one end of the wire through the center of a sweater square. Continue adding squares until you have a colorful wreath. The sweater pieces should be very tightly packed onto the wire frame.

3. When you have finished the wreath, twist the ends of the hanger back together. Using the wire cutters, remove any extra length of wire. Close the gap by pushing sweater pieces together over it.

4. From the reserved arm, cut a piece of sweater 10 to 12 inches/25 to 30.5 cm long and 1 to 1½ inches/2.5 to 3.5 cm wide. Make a bow and, with the needle and thread, sew the bow onto the top of the wreath. Cut away the ends of the bow if they are too long.

herb wreath

An herb wreath is an unusual twist on the traditional holiday wreath and a welcome addition to any cook's kitchen. Not only is it pretty, it's fun to pinch herbs from it for a winter soup. Because not all herbs are in season during the winter months—for example, basil, parsley, and marjoram—plan ahead and dry your herbs in the autumn. Do not use brittle or over-dried herbs, because they will break and will have to be discarded. A dry but flexible herb is the easiest to work with.

To dry the herbs, tie them in small bunches and hang them (outside, if weather permits) from a clothesline for two to three days. If you must hang them inside, the kitchen is the best place, because it is usually warm and dry. Store the dried herbs in reused freezer bags or sealed containers in the freezer.

- **An assortment of fresh and pre-dried herbs, such as thyme, rosemary, oregano, marjoram, spearmint, bay leaves, flat-leaf parsley, sage (see Note)**

- **1 wreath frame, 7 inches/17 cm in diameter**

- **1 roll of 24-gauge florist wire (preferably green coated)**

- **Wire cutters**

1. Decide which herbs you plan to use. Many herbs do not have to be pre-dried. Fresh bunches of rosemary, oregano, marjoram, and mint will dry perfectly on the wreath. Bay leaves, flat-leaf parsley, and sage must be pre-dried. (Dried bay leaves can be purchased at the grocery store.)

2. Place each herb in a separate bundle approximately 3 inches/8 cm wide at the head, or flowered, area of the herbs. (The bunches should be approximately 3 inches/8 cm in diameter at the head and the stems approximately 5 inches/13 cm long.)

3. Beginning at the top of the wreath frame, secure an herb bundle to the frame with the wire. Layer the next bunch over the first, so that the head of the second overlaps the stems of the first, and secure it with the wire. Continue adding bunches, following the wreath form, until all areas are filled and all the herb bunches are used up. Make the wreath as full as possible; the herbs will shrink as they dry, so the fuller, the better. The wreath will dry out in about a week; it will last for about six weeks before the herbs lose their taste and aroma. You can pull the wreath apart and place the herbs in a jar after a month.

NOTE: *You will need ten to twenty herb bunches to assemble a 7-inch/17-cm wreath. If you cannot obtain that many herbs, you can scale down: wreath frames come in a variety of sizes.*

newspaper stocking

These stockings are sturdy enough to hold a few holiday items, but don't fill them with too much stuff! Remember, the whole point is not to buy too much stuff anyway.

- **Four sheets of Christmas-themed newspaper (ads, articles, or any festive images) or used wrapping paper**
- **Scissors**
- **Needle and thread**
- **Glue**
- **Beads, small bells, faux fur, cashmere or fabric scraps, vintage buttons, recycled glass pieces, seashells, decorative images cut from holiday cards or magazines**

1. Fold the four sheets of newspaper into 8 layers (8 layers will make a sturdy stocking) that are still at least 12 by 10 inches/ 30.5 by 25 cm in size. With the scissors, cut a stocking shape out of the paper in your desired size. (You can always place a cloth stocking on the newspaper and trace around it to create the shape.)

2. Using the needle and thread, hand stitch the outer edges of the stocking together, leaving the top open.

3. Glue on any extra holiday images to decorate the stocking

4. Layer the remaining four pieces of scrap newspaper and cut them into strips 1 inch/2.5 cm wide by 4 inches/10 cm long. Stack them and create a loop.

5. Sew or staple the loop to the inner top edge of the stocking, to hang it.

6. Glue whatever trimmings you've gathered to the top of the stocking (be sure to cover the stitches or staples from the loop). Add bells and other embellishments.

MAKE THE YULE LOG A GREEN LOG

Cozying up in front of a roaring fire is a holiday tradition for many, but sadly, it isn't a very green one. Thankfully, nowadays we have earth-friendly choices we can make if we don't want to completely abandon the treasured fire.

Choosing the right kind of fireplace can be the first step. Gas and wood fireplaces are the most common, but the greenest choice is the pellet stove. These stoves burn a renewable fuel made of ground dried wood and corn, compressed into pellets. The pellets are poured into the stove and burn for up to twenty-four hours. Pellet stoves are some of the cleanest-burning heating appliances available today (so clean, in fact, that they are exempt from EPA air-quality certification) and are very energy efficient. Pellet stoves do require electricity to run their fans, however (100 kilowatt hours per month), and depending on where you live, the pellets can be hard to find.

That crackling wood fire may smell wonderful, but with every crackle, particulates are emitted into the atmosphere, affecting air quality both indoors and out. Smoke exposure has been linked to asthma and bronchitis, among other respiratory ailments. What's more, the heat generated by traditional fireplaces is inefficient. One option to reduce heat-waste is to install a stainless steel insert in the chimney, which will prevent heat from getting trapped in the masonry or pulled outside (so it actually will heat the house).

The good news? Burning wood does not contribute to global warming, which is caused primarily by burning fossil fuels (they release CO_2 that would not otherwise be in the atmosphere). Wood stoves, made of cast-iron or stone, have a low particulate output because of government standards (each state sets its own requirements for limiting particulate emissions), and they are effective for heating small areas.

Gas fireplaces lack the aroma of burning wood but generate enough heat to warm a room. The environmental dilemma with gas fireplaces is that they burn natural gas or propane, which are fossil fuels. Unvented gas fireplaces emit nitrogen dioxide and carbon monoxide and are a source of indoor air pollution. But they do emit fewer particulates overall: thirty houses with wood-burning fireplaces create as much particulate pollution as thirty thousand houses with gas fireplaces. If you're choosing between a traditional wood-burning fireplace and a new gas fireplace, the more energy-efficient gas fireplace is the greener choice.

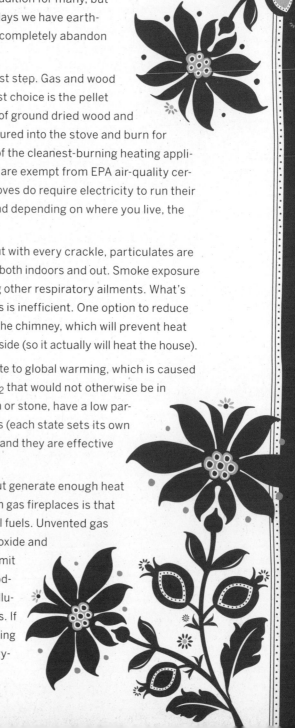

Electric "logs" are another option. Made from ceramic, they flicker like a real fire and give off as much heat as a small space heater. But of course, they are powered by electricity.

Ethanol gel fireplaces are some of the newest fireplaces to hit the market, and some people consider them the greenest of all. They're smokeless, because they run on ethanol derived from corn or sugarcane, and they require no vent, because they emit only water vapor and a tiny amount of CO_2. They won't heat a room, but they will give you the sense of a fireplace with a real flame.

If you do use a wood-burning fireplace, here are a few things you can do to reduce its environmental impact:

- Get your chimney cleaned once a year.

- Burn only hardwood, such as oak, eucalyptus, or hickory, which give off more heat than other types of wood, making them a more efficient choice. Never burn trash or plastics, which emit toxic fumes.

- Think about where the logs are coming from and buy local if possible.

- The absolute greenest option is to skip the wood entirely and buy eco-logs (see page 172).

- Plant a tree for every fire that you light (see Resources).

| HOLIDAY ENERGY EFFICIENCY |

When the temperature drops, most people turn up the thermostat without a thought. But you can stay cozy this winter while being energy efficient. Here are some ways to cut energy costs across all aspects of your life at home.

- Turn down the thermostat to 68 degrees Fahrenheit (20 degrees Celsius). Check to see if there are gaps around windows or doors, and caulk them. Dress warmly and keep doors closed.

- Set your Christmas tree lights on a timer. (For more on holiday lights, see page 32.)

- If you are renovating your house and can afford it, install radiant floor heating; its thermostat can be lowered 2 to 4 degrees and still keep your house as warm as conventional heating systems, and that results in a 10 to 40 percent reduction in energy costs.

- Minimize your ice use. You don't need too many ice-cold drinks in the winter, and some nutritionists say ice is not good for your digestive system anyway. Plus, constantly opening and closing the freezer door wastes electricity. Use ice during holiday parties only. And drink more Chai Hot Cocoa! (See page 115.)

- Fill up your refrigerator. It takes less energy to keep a lot of things cold than it does to keep a few things cold.

LED light balls

Add twinkling lights to your holiday table: simply roll strands of LED Christmas tree lights into tightly wrapped balls (similar to a rubber band ball) and place them in glass jars or bowls. (Just be sure the display is near an electrical outlet.) For extra drama, place the light balls in a clear glass vase or under a bell jar. To hide the cord, cut a small hole in the tablecloth and run the cord under the tablecloth to the outlet.

| TWINKLE THE RIGHT WAY |

Switch out those holiday lights: LED lights (LED stands for "light-emitting diode," the same technology that powers your computer) use 90 percent less energy than traditional holiday lights. They last for up to twenty years and burn as long as a hundred thousand hours, according to Energy Star. Available in many colors and sizes, they also emit less heat than standard holiday lights, so they are less of a fire danger, and they don't contain mercury or other toxic chemicals. Another plus: when one light on a strand goes out, the others stay lit. (Solar-powered LEDs are also available in some areas.)

LED lights do cost a bit more than standard lights but will pay for themselves in one to two seasons. In fact, if half of all traditional Christmas bulbs were replaced with LED bulbs, it could yield a savings of seventeen billion dollars a year in energy bills, according to HowStuffWorks.com. If you want something more than just strings of lights, look for decorative reindeer made with LED lights (see Resources).

And be sure to set your lights on a timer, or turn them off when you go to sleep; the tree doesn't need to stay lit all night long.

bell jar mini scene

Sometimes the simplest Christmas decorations are the most beautiful. You can create your own perfect holiday scene using a bell jar or the glass shade from a hurricane lamp and a few festive objects. These scenes look particularly nice on top of an entryway table, console, or piano. If you don't have a bell jar on hand, arrange the scene on a windowsill. Vintage bell jars are available on eBay as well at flea markets.

GATHER

CREATE

- **1 bell jar or glass shade from a hurricane lamp**

- **An array of decorative Christmas items, such as juniper berries, star anise, vintage Christmas collectibles, pinecones, glittered twigs, feathers, and other memorabilia**

- **Votive candle (optional)**

This is a perfect craft to let your imagination run wild. Arrange the items on a flat surface in a fun and creative way, in a space small enough for the bell jar or hurricane glass to cover. Then cover the scene and place it where you and others can enjoy it.

| ANOTHER OPTION |

To make snowy scenes, collect different size glass jars (old jam jars or other sorts of jars) and fill them one-third to half full with sugar or salt. Place found objects such as tiny vintage Christmas trees or deer figurines in the jars to create little winter scenes. Put a small votive candle and a few pieces of star anise in another jar, and arrange them all on a table.

| SALT OR SUGAR SCRUB |

Instead of throwing away the salt or sugar you used for the Christmas jar scenes, make a body scrub. There is nothing like a nice scrub to leave your dry winter skin silky smooth, and it makes a great gift.

1 cup/200 g sugar or salt

1/2 cup/120 ml olive oil or sesame oil

3 to 4 drops essential oil (lavender for relaxing, citrus oil for invigorating, or any essential oil you like)

Mix the sugar or salt, olive oil, and essential oil together in a glass jar and close tightly.

silver leaf wire window ornaments

These fun silvery wire-leaf strands look like magical icicles hanging in the window. Play with the length: they can be long or short, depending on the size of your window. They look beautiful hanging in French doors or in any doorway, or lay them on tabletops for dinner party decorations. Best is to collect fallen leaves from the woods or your garden for this decoration, but leaves are also available for sale at most flower shops and craft stores.

GATHER

- **Nontoxic water-based silver paint**
- **Small paintbrush**
- **20 leaves of various shapes and sizes (they should be no longer than 5 inches/13cm each for 8 feet/244 cm of wire)**
- **Sheets of newspaper**
- **1 roll of 26-gauge silver wire**
- **Wire cutters**

CREATE

1. Paint both sides of each leaf silver and allow the leaves to dry on the newspaper. While they are drying, measure the length of the window you wish to decorate. Add an additional ¼ inch/6.5 mm, and cut the wire to this length.

2. Starting 2 to 3 inches/5 to 8 cm from one end, wrap the wire tightly around the leaf stem several times (at least five), and bend the wire that remains so it is parallel to end of the leaf. Bend the leaf to the left so that not all the leaves are facing in the same direction.

3. Approximately 2 to 3 inches/5 to 8 cm down from the first leaf, wind the wire several times around the stem of the second leaf, and then bend the leaf to the right.

4. Repeat with the remaining leaves, alternately bending the leaves to the left and right. Cut off any excess wire with the wire cutters.

GLOBAL GREEN:

Christmas in Italy (Buon Natale)

Christmas is wildly popular in Italy, and Italians set many green examples, starting with their decorations. Rather than elaborate energy-wasting light displays, holiday decorations in Italy are primarily focused on the Nativity scene, *presepi*, which is set up in every church and in many outdoor spaces. Families gather for Christmas Eve dinner, which in most regions consists mainly of fish—as many as ten or twelve dishes—followed by midnight mass. Italy is also the third-largest producer of organic food in Europe.

LET IT SNOW!

A white Christmas fulfills a holiday dream for many, but never force nature's hand with artificial snow sprays to decorate a wreath or window. Although some companies make nontoxic sprays, many sprays still contain the carcinogen dichloromethane. And large stick-on snowflake decals can be a choking hazard for small children. Instead, how about making your own snowflakes by cutting them out from used wrapping paper, tissue paper, or doilies? You can hang them in the window or from the ceiling in your entryway.

WHEN FROSTY *isn't* SO FROSTY

Sledding, skiing, and building snowmen are wonderful winter pastimes, but as global warming progresses, warmer winters are a significant trend, threatening our planet as well as our favorite winter activities. A study published by climate scientists in the journal *Science* in 2008 used statistical modeling to confirm that mountains in the United States are receiving more rain and less snow, with more rivers running dry in summer. For the first time, scientists were able to directly link these climate changes to the increased greenhouse gases in the atmosphere. A NASA study found that 2007 was the warmest winter on record. And it's not just Americans who will miss those snowy Christmas mornings: BBC News reported that climate change research indicates snowfall will decrease dramatically in Britain by 2080. Now is our opportunity to make a difference. If a friend or family member is reluctant to give up a few favorite holiday traditions to help the planet, remind him or her how climate change will directly affect his or her life; in this case, it might mean fewer days on the ski slopes.

To share information like this with my family members, I send them Web links about global warming. They can read up on it themselves and decide how they want to make a change. My intent is not to scare them. In fact, I try not to overemphasize my own beliefs about the dangers of climate change; rather, I try to just inspire people by setting an example with my own choices.

EXPERT GREEN TIP

RACHEL LINCOLN SARNOFF, *founder, EcoStiletto*
www.ecostiletto.com

For my family, the holidays begin in November. Because we're scattered around the country from Santa Fe to New Orleans, and because all our children want Santa to come down their own chimneys Christmas morning, we try to meet at my house every year for a huge Thanksgiving dinner. We add foldout table to foldout table until it basically stretches from the front door to the kitchen. Beforehand, we all get in the holiday spirit by cutting out paper snowflakes from leftover newspapers—especially the brightly colored toy mailers and comics. The younger kids make just a few nicks and cuts, the rest of us compete to see who can make the most intricate design, but we're all amazed when we open up our folded up paper and a beautiful pattern emerges. We tape them to the insides of the windows, with the kids directing the placement, then gather outside the house to view its transformation. It's truly my favorite event of the season: Making something beautiful from what is essentially trash. The tradition costs virtually nothing, gives us an opportunity to talk and laugh and catch up while we're doing it, and reminds us of our incredible, colorful, diverse family every time we look through our windows.

EXPERT GREEN TIP

DARREN MOORE, *founder, Ecovations; co-host, "Alter Eco" on Planet Green*
www.ecovations.com

If you want to have a "green" home, have it Energy Star Home Performance tested. The testing could cut energy consumption in half, while drastically improving comfort in your home. An Energy Star Home Performance Contractor will conduct a range of tests using equipment that can see the movement of temperature through the walls to check your home's energy efficiency, comfort, and safety. Those tests, plus a look at your energy bills, will tell you which steps will be most effective in making improvements to your home.

chandelier-gem branch bouquet

Instead of buying cut flowers to decorate your home, most of which have been imported from other countries and sprayed with chemicals, make your own magical all-natural bouquets from branches. Collect fallen branches from the woods, or call around to florists to ask if they carry any. (During the holiday season, florists often add branches to floral arrangements, and you can buy a bunch for a good price.) Farmers' markets also are good sources. Look for old chandelier pieces at a flea market or secondhand shop. Better yet, if you have an old chandelier that has been exiled to the garage, now is the time to get it and pull it apart.

GATHER

CREATE

- 6 to 8 branches (red willow, manzanita, and birch branches are beautiful and sturdy)

- Tall glass vase, 14 to 16 inches/ 35 to 40 cm high

- 5 or 6 lengths of used ribbon, 5 inches/13 cm long (velvet is especially pretty)

- 5 to 6 strands of chandelier gems, each 4 to 5 inches/10 to 13 cm long

1. Arrange the branches in the vase in a pretty way.

2. Using the ribbon, tie the chandelier pieces onto the various branches, staggering them decoratively.

| GLITTERED TWIGS |

Giving plain twigs a holiday sparkle is easy. Gather different leafless twigs (preferably ones that have fallen from trees). Place nontoxic glue on random spots on a twig (or cover the entire twig with glue), then sprinkle nontoxic glitter over it. (White iridescent glitter or silver look very snowlike.) Let dry. Place the twigs in bunches to decorate the table for a dinner party, add them to a Bell Jar Mini Scene (see page 33), or incorporate them into your tree decorations.

glittered fruit cornucopia

I like to fill vintage Moroccan bowls with glittery winter fruits such as pomegranates, persimmons, and mandarins. They make very festive arrangements. Plus, once you remove the glittered exterior, you can eat most of the hard-skinned fruits so nothing goes to waste.

GATHER

CREATE

Gather a nontoxic glue stick; various fresh fruits, such as persimmons, crabapples, pomegranates, mandarins, or tangerines; and nontoxic silver or gold glitter. You also can include nuts in their shells, such as walnuts or Brazil nuts.

Using the glue stick, gently dab random spots of glue onto the pieces of fruit. Sprinkle the glitter over the glue, and allow to dry. Place the fruit in a pretty bowl on a table or sideboard. If you like, add nuts to the arrangement.

| THE HOLLY AND THE IVY |

Before you bring holiday plants into your home, make sure to check if they're safe. Although it's romantic, that piece of mistletoe is actually poisonous, so if you must have it, hang it high and make sure it's securely out of the reach of children and pets. Holly berries are also poisonous, so keep them out of reach too, or skip them altogether. Poinsettias often turn up on poisonous-plant lists, but according to the Society of American Florists, they're actually nontoxic. Some festive and nontoxic plants to give or display this Christmas include African violets, jade plants, Christmas cactus, and orchids. But again, remember to act locally when choosing plants.

EXPERT GREEN TIP
DEBBIE LEVIN, CEO,
the Environmental Media Association
www.ema.org

One of my favorite green-holiday ideas is to send e-cards instead of mailing holiday cards. It's actually much easier, because we have so many e-mail addresses and not always snail mail addresses! I think it's a creative alternative that not only saves paper and stamps, but is economical as well.

Another thing I like to do is to find antique decorations. They're always so much more interesting anyway!

The day after your holiday dinner, skip the turkey sandwich and donate your leftovers to a shelter.

truffled goat cheese macaroni and cheese

Who doesn't love a warm plate of delicious, creamy macaroni and cheese? I have changed the classic all-American dish around a bit to give it a holiday flair. Multiple varieties of goat cheese add a sophisticated flavor, and the truffle salt gives this dish the perfect festive touch. I have made it countless times, and everybody, young and old alike, finishes every last morsel.

Always look for local cheese and other dairy products. Cypress Grove makes a wide variety of goat cheeses. Truffles, which once came only from Italy and France, are now often from Oregon. I use Italian truffle salt in this recipe, which is available online and in specialty shops, but a more sustainable (and more exotic) option is to order fresh truffles from Oregon (see Resources), leave out the truffle salt, and shave fresh truffles right onto the mac and cheese as it comes out of the oven; the aroma and flavor are divine.

| SERVES 6 TO 8 |

- 1 pound/450 g elbow macaroni
- 4½ cups/1 L whole milk
- 7 tablespoons unsalted butter
- 5 tablespoons all-purpose flour
- 1½ teaspoons truffle salt
- 8 ounces/225 g fresh soft goat's milk cheese at room temperature
- 6 ounces/170 g (about 1¾ cups) grated goat's milk cheddar as well as any other hard, aged goat cheese
- Salt and pepper to taste
- 1 tablespoon minced garlic
- 1½ cups/75 g panko crumbs (or any bread crumbs)

1. Preheat the oven to 350°F/180°C (Gas Mark 4).

2. Bring a large pot of salted water to a boil. Add the macaroni and cook until al dente, according to manufacturer's directions. It's very important to slightly undercook the pasta, so it doesn't get too soft during baking. Drain the pasta and set aside.

3. Warm the milk in a medium pot over low heat and set aside.

4. In a large pot over medium heat, make a roux by melting 5 tablespoons of butter and then adding the flour, stirring constantly until the butter and flour are combined. Lower the heat and cook for about 3 minutes more, stirring constantly, until the flour mixture releases a nutty aroma. Stir in the truffle salt.

5. Using a large ladle, add the warm milk to the roux one ladleful at a time, stirring till combined between each addition, until all the milk has been added. Add the soft goat's milk cheese and stir until combined. Gradually add ¾ cup (2.5 oz./75 g) of the grated cheese, stirring the milk mixture constantly and rapidly until the cheese has melted.

6. When the cheese has completely melted, season to taste with salt and pepper and add the macaroni. Stir until the macaroni is well coated and transfer to an 8-by-11-inch/20-by-27-cm baking dish.

7. In a saucepan, melt the remaining 2 tablespoons butter over medium heat. Add the garlic and sauté for 1 minute. Add the panko crumbs and sauté until lightly browned, about 1 minute.

8. Sprinkle the remaining grated cheese on the macaroni, and then sprinkle the panko crumbs on top.

9. Bake on the middle rack of the oven, uncovered, for 25 to 30 minutes, until bubbly and lightly brown on top. Let the macaroni and cheese cool for 5 to 10 minutes before serving.

| GO ORGANIC! STAY LOCAL! |

When you're planning a Christmas dinner or holiday party, it's a great opportunity to choose organic: not only does organic food taste better, it's better for us and better for the planet. Whether you're selecting a turkey, a bag of apples, or a bunch of parsley, there are a number of good reasons to go organic and buy locally:

- Organic farming practices don't use chemical pesticides, insecticides, herbicides, or fertilizers, thereby contributing to the overall quality of the soil, air, and water, as well as our own health.

- Supporting local organic farmers helps reduce energy consumption. Overall energy use on conventional farms is much greater than on organic farms, because of their reliance on nitrogen fertilizers and pesticides.

- Organic produce has levels of antioxidants 30 percent higher than its conventional counterpart.

- If you're buying seasonal, you're buying local; the average meal travels twelve hundred miles from farm to your home.

Shopping seasonally and locally also saves fuel and other energy costs because it does not require the food to be trucked in from far-away places. Commit yourself to the four-hundred-mile challenge, in which all the food you buy comes from within a four-hundred-mile radius. It's a great way to be green in your kitchen and your community. Check out the Natural Resources Defense Council's link on eating locally; you can plug in your zip code to find growers near you: www.nrdc.org/health/foodmiles.

BORROW A TRADITION

Here are a few examples of ways some families have incorporated green changes into their holiday celebrations; perhaps they will inspire you to do the same.

My mother inspired similar traditions in our house; every year before Christmas, my brother and I went through our toys and chose "gently worn" ones to donate to charity. This resonated with me, because the less we had, the more we appreciated. We also became more creative: one year we used old sheets to make a fort, and we got reacquainted with our art supplies. Traditions like this show that the Christmas spirit is coming from a place of real gratitude and demonstrate that it's a duty and a pleasure to share with others. I've continued this tradition with my daughter; it's important to be able to start that dialogue with your children when they're at a young age. If you do give away toys, be sure to start the process before Christmas, because most charities need the toys for Christmas Day. If you can't find an organization that accepts gently used toys, contact a local church, preschool, hospital, or homeless shelter, which often are in need of toys.

Here are some other ideas:

- Make it a family project to create Christmas cards out of recycled paper, instead of buying new ones.

- Decorate a living Christmas tree, outside or inside, instead of buying a cut tree.

- Personalize and reuse your wrapping paper every year, so that each person has a special wrapping paper for his or her gifts.

- Turn off the TV during the holiday season and play board games or work on art projects instead. You'll save energy and also encourage family time.

- Arrange a cookie swap with two or three other families, instead of exchanging presents.

sweet potato christmas enchiladas

My Swedish friend Shandra, who grew up in New Mexico, appeared at my Christmas Eve potluck party one year with a platter of these enchiladas, garnished with pomegranate seeds. They were a hit. Garnish with an additional handful of chopped cilantro for a festive red and green touch. (If you happen to have a friend who will be visiting New Mexico, ask him or her to bring you back a bag of New Mexico Hatch green chiles. New Mexico is famous for them.)

| SERVES 6 TO 8 |

FOR THE GREEN CHILE SAUCE

- 2 pounds/900 g Anaheim or Pasilla chiles, roasted, peeled, and seeded (see Note)
- 2 cloves garlic, finely chopped
- 1½ cups/230 g chopped yellow onion
- 2 tablespoons olive oil
- 2 tablespoons all-purpose flour
- 1 teaspoon ground cumin
- 2 vegetable bouillon cubes
- 1½ cups/375 ml water
- Salt and pepper to taste
- 2 teaspoons sugar

FOR THE RED CHILE SAUCE

- 1 tablespoon olive oil
- 1 clove garlic, minced
- 3 heaping tablespoons red chili powder
- 2 tablespoons all-purpose flour

- ½ teaspoon ground cumin
- 2 vegetable bouillon cubes
- 2 cups/500 ml water
- Salt to taste

FOR THE ENCHILADAS

- ½ cup/120 ml plus 2 tablespoons olive oil
- 18 corn tortillas (2 packages)
- 5 medium sweet potatoes, cooked and mashed
- 24 ounces/660 g Monterey Jack cheese, shredded
- 1 cup/15 g chopped fresh cilantro, for garnish
- 2 cups/16 oz. sour cream, for garnish
- 1 cup/270 g pomegranate seeds, for garnish

TO MAKE THE GREEN CHILE SAUCE:

1. Place the chiles in the bowl of a food processor and pulse until smooth.

2. In a medium pot over medium heat, sauté the garlic and onion in the oil until the onion is translucent, 3 to 4 minutes.

3. Add the chiles, stir, and cook 3 minutes more.

4. Add the flour and cumin, stir, reduce heat to low, and cook for 3 minutes.

5. Add the bouillon cubes, then slowly add the water to dissolve the cubes. Add the salt, pepper, and sugar and simmer for 10 minutes.

TO MAKE THE RED CHILE SAUCE:

1. Heat the olive oil in a small saucepan over medium heat and sauté the garlic for 1 minute.

2. Add the chili powder and stir to make a paste.

3. Add the flour and cumin and cook for 2 minutes, stirring constantly.

4. Add the bouillon cubes and slowly add the water to dissolve the cubes. Whisk to break up any lumps. Add the salt, bring the sauce to a boil, then lower the heat and simmer until thick, about 10 to 12 minutes. Strain through a fine-mesh sieve. Set aside.

TO MAKE THE ENCHILADAS:

1. Preheat the oven to 350°F/180°C (Gas Mark 4).

2. Heat ½ cup/120 ml olive oil in a skillet over medium-high heat. Place a tortilla in the oil and quickly turn it until both sides are lightly coated, then place it on a towel to absorb the excess oil. Repeat for each tortilla.

3. Place a layer of tortillas flat in a 9-by-12 inch/23-by-30.5 cm glass casserole dish. Smear a layer of mashed sweet potatoes on the tortillas, followed by a layer of cheese, and then a layer of green chile sauce, followed by another layer of tortillas. Repeat the layering with remaining ingredients (except the red chile sauce), ending with a layer of cheese.

4. Bake the enchiladas uncovered for 25 minutes, or until bubbly. Garnish with the cilantro, sour cream, and pomegranate seeds, and serve hot with the red chile sauce on the side.

NOTE: *To roast the chiles, place them directly on a gas flame and keep turning them until they are completely black. Place the blackened chiles in a pot or glass or stainless steel bowl, cover, and let them sweat on the counter for 30 minutes. Peel off the blackened skins and remove the seeds. If you have an electric stove, preheat the broiler to high and set the oven rack as close to the broiler as possible. Place the chiles on a cookie sheet and put them in the broiler, leaving the door slightly ajar. Broil for 5 to 10 minutes, turning every few minutes, until the skins are charred and blistered. (Don't leave the peppers unattended; there's a very small chance they could catch fire.) Place the blackened chiles in a pot, cover, and let them sweat for 30 minutes. Peel off the blackened skins and remove the seeds.*

EXPERT GREEN TIP

JEFFREY HOLLENDER, *president and chief inspired protagonist, Seventh Generation*

Our celebrations start at Thanksgiving, which is my favorite holiday because we give thanks not gifts. It's a reflective time, and trying to find new ways to show our appreciation is always a pleasure. I traditionally do a dinner reading that expresses my feelings, and I like the challenge of unearthing the right piece. We also use our holiday meals to express our beliefs in sustainability, which we do by focusing on cooking local organic foods throughout the season.

roasted acorn squash soup with parmesan and crispy sage

Dark green, yellow, or gold acorn squash are among winter's best vegetables, with their sweet, rich, nutty flavor. This comforting soup can start off a holiday meal or be served on its own on a cold winter evening.

| SERVES 6 TO 8 |

- 3 pounds/1.35 kg acorn squash, peeled, seeded, and cut into 1-inch/2.5 cm cubes (see Note)
- Salt to taste
- 4 tablespoons olive oil
- 1 carrot, roughly chopped
- 1 rib celery, roughly chopped
- 1 leek (white part only), roughly chopped
- ½ medium white or yellow onion, roughly chopped
- 6 cups/1.5 L chicken broth
- ¼ teaspoon white pepper
- ⅛ teaspoon nutmeg
- ⅛ teaspoon ground cinnamon
- 12 fresh sage leaves
- Parmesan cheese, for garnish

1. Preheat the oven to 375°F/190°C (Gas Mark 5). Lightly oil a baking sheet.

2. Place the squash on the baking sheet, sprinkle with salt, and bake for 30 to 35 minutes, until soft. Set aside.

3. Heat 2 tablespoons olive oil in a large pot over medium heat. Add the carrot, celery, leek, and onion and cook for 5 minutes, stirring occasionally, until the onions are translucent. Add the broth and cook for 30 to 35 minutes, uncovered, until the carrots are soft. Add the squash and cook for 5 more minutes. Add the white pepper, nutmeg, and cinnamon.

4. Transfer the soup to a blender and puree in batches if necessary, then return the pureed soup to the pot. Or, use an immersion blender and puree the soup in the pot.

5. Heat the remaining 2 tablespoons olive oil in a medium saucepan over medium-high heat. Add the sage leaves and fry until the leaves turn dark green, about 2 minutes. Serve hot, garnished with crispy sage leaves and a sprinkling of Parmesan.

NOTE: *If you can't find acorn squash, butternut will work in a pinch.*

endive, radicchio, arugula, and pear salad with candied ginger, goat cheese, and spiced walnuts

Pears, a quintessential winter fruit, bring both color and flavor to this perfect holiday salad. The candied ginger, goat cheese, and spiced nuts add some excitement to its traditional Italian flavors. Shopping seasonally and, of course, locally whenever possible saves fuel, water, and other energy costs from not having food trucked in from far away places. Check out the Natural Resources Defense Council's link on eating locally; you can actually plug in your zip code to find local growers near you: www.nrdc.org/health/foodmiles.

| SERVES 6 TO 8 |

FOR THE SPICED WALNUTS

- 2 tablespoons unsalted butter
- 1 cup/125 g walnut pieces
- 3 tablespoons brown sugar
- ½ teaspoon ground cinnamon
- ¾ teaspoon ground cumin
- ¼ teaspoon salt

FOR THE BALSAMIC DRESSING

- 2¼ tablespoons balsamic vinegar
- ¾ teaspoon agave nectar or honey
- ½ teaspoon salt
- ½ teaspoon freshly ground pepper
- 4½ tablespoons extra-virgin olive oil

FOR THE SALAD

- 4 ounces/120 g soft goat cheese, at room temperature
- 2 teaspoons candied ginger, finely chopped
- 5 to 6 ounces/150 to 170 g baby arugula
- 3 heads Belgian endive, finely sliced
- 1 small head radicchio, finely sliced
- 2 small firm but ripe pears, finely sliced
- Pomegranate seeds, for garnish

TO MAKE THE SPICED WALNUTS:

1. Preheat the oven to 375°F/190°C (Gas Mark 5). Line a baking sheet with parchment paper.

2. Melt the butter in a small saucepan. Stir in the walnuts, remove the pan from heat, and continue stirring until walnuts are completely coated in butter.

3. Transfer the walnuts to a medium bowl and add the brown sugar, cumin, cinnamon, and salt. Stir until well mixed.

4. Transfer the walnuts to the prepared baking sheet and bake for 10 minutes.

5. Remove the walnuts from the oven and let cool.

TO MAKE THE BALSAMIC DRESSING:

1. In a small bowl, stir together the vinegar, agave nectar or honey, salt, and pepper until well blended.

2. Whisk in the olive oil until mixture has emulsified.

TO MAKE THE SALAD:

1. In a small bowl, combine the goat cheese and candied ginger. Cover and place in the refrigerator for 30 minutes, or until ready to serve.

2. To assemble the salad, place the arugula, endive, radicchio, and pear slices in a medium bowl. Pour the dressing over the top and gently toss until evenly coated.

3. Place the salad on individual plates and crumble the goat cheese and ginger evenly over each. Top with spiced walnuts and pomegranate seeds.

entertaining

Celebrations are an integral part of the holidays, whether it's sharing meals with family or opening your home to neighbors and friends. Entertaining is a way to catch up with old friends and **rejuvenate** the soul.

I find myself in the kitchen for much of the Christmas season, and my easy, healthful, **festive** recipes—which I share with you in this book—make entertaining a little less stressful. (And most of the recipes can be prepared ahead of time, to cut down on last-minute preparation.) But the meal doesn't end with the food: setting a Christmas table is a joyful **tradition** as well, and it's even more fun with a few homemade elements, such as name-card holders and centerpieces.

And of course, dinner parties and cocktail parties aren't the only ways to connect with friends. Host an afternoon cookie-decorating party; the adults can catch up over a glass of wine and an appetizer while the kids decorate cookies and drink hot cocoa. Afternoon open houses or brunches are other ways to host people during this busy season, and they require just a few menu items. Remember, **connecting** with the people you love is more important than creating the perfect holiday buffet.

For invitations, skip the paper invites (save trees and postage!) and send an e-mail or Evite (www.evite.com), or, pick up the phone instead.

Party favors are another festive touch at a holiday gathering, and it's easy to keep them green: give guests boxes of organic chocolate or homemade cookies (wrapped in reused containers, of course) or crafts that your children have created. Ideas abound in this chapter.

star anise napkin holders

Dip into the kitchen spice cabinet to create these charming napkin holders. Star anise is the seedpod of an evergreen tree native to Vietnam and China. It has a beautiful shape and lends itself perfectly to these festive Christmas napkin holders.

| MAKES 6 NAPKIN HOLDERS |

GATHER

- 1 roll of 24-gauge silver wire
- Wire cutters
- 30 star anise pods
- 30 crystal beads

CREATE

1. Cut six 8-inch/20-cm lengths of silver wire. A ½ inch/1.25 cm down one length of wire, place the back side of a star anise pod against the wire and wrap the long end of the wire once around it. Twist both ends of the wire to secure.

2. String one crystal bead onto the wire all the way up to the top and center of the star anise. Wrap the wire again around the star anise.

3. Space approximately 1 inch/2.5 cm of wire in between the first star anise pod and a second.

4. Repeat steps 1, 2, and 3 five times (you'll use 5 star anise for each napkin holder).

5. Take both loose ends of wire and wrap them around the bottom wire of the last star anise twice to secure, creating a circle.

6. Cut away the excess wire.

| SUPER-EASY NAPKIN RINGS |

I am always looking for good uses for the extra gift ribbons I have lying around, and this is one of my favorites. Gather the prettiest ribbons you have and cut them into 10-inch/25-cm lengths. Assemble the ribbons into bunches of three and tie them tightly around hemp or organic linen napkins that have been folded twice and rolled up.

GREEN PARTY TIP

We tend to generate more waste when we throw a party, so instead of using the usual plastic garbage bags for trash, choose bags made from recycled material, or BioBags, which are made from non-GMO corn. BioBags are 100 percent recyclable and compostable (see Resources). According to Seventh Generation, if every household in the United States replaced one thirty-count package of virgin plastic kitchen bags with 55 percent recycled-plastic bags, we could save forty-nine thousand barrels of oil, enough to heat and cool twenty-eight hundred homes in the United States for one year.

STUDDED "FRUIT"

A few years ago at a flea market I found vintage imitation studded fruits, including apples, pears, lemons, oranges, and grapes. Apparently, in the 1960s and 1970s, women used to sit around and make these lovely decorations. They would start with Styrofoam fruit shapes and stud them with glass or plastic beads. The decorations are charming and will last forever. Studded fruits look great in a big glass bowl or arranged on a tree amid vintage ball ornaments. They also look great placed randomly on a Christmas dinner table. Studded fruits are still widely available at flea markets, thrift shops, and on auction web sites. Ask your aunt or grandmother if she has any in a box in an attic somewhere—if the answer is yes, you will have struck gold.

DRYING POMEGRANATES

Select fresh pomegranates free of bruises and cracks. Space them at least 2 inches/5 cm apart on a wire rack, so that the air can circulate around them. Leave the pomegranates in your pantry or kitchen closet for several weeks. The pomegranates will dry by releasing moisture through their crowns. Dried whole pomegranates can last for up to two years.

THE PARTY LINE ON CLOTH *vs.* PAPER NAPKINS

Napkins are a must for any holiday party, but this year, swap out paper napkins and use cloth instead. (The same goes for tablecloths.) Those colorful paper napkins aren't recyclable, and although they look pretty, they use virgin wood and contain chemical dyes.

I grew up with cloth napkins. Whenever we visited my grandmother, we each had our own napkin ring, and we used the same napkin for the entire week. To wash cloth napkins in an eco-friendly manner, soak them in a nontoxic hydrogen-peroxide-based bleach and eco-friendly laundry detergent and then wash them in cold water. Hang them on a clothesline to dry. (An indoor clothes-line set up in a basement or attic warmed by the water heater is ideal.) When choosing cloth napkins, look for those made from organic cotton, hemp, or linen (see Resources). Instead of buying new cloth napkins, purchasing vintage ones from a thrift or antique store is even greener.

If you must use paper napkins, look for ones made from recycled paper. There are two main types of recycled content in paper products: postconsumer fiber and recovered fiber. Postconsumer fiber comes from paper that has already been used; recovered fiber is from paper waste left over from manufacturing. When buying recycled paper products, look for 100 percent recycled paper with a minimum of 90 percent postconsumer content. Remember, the higher the postconsumer percentage, the more paper is being kept out of a landfill. If every household in the United States replaced just one package of virgin-fiber napkins with 100 percent recycled ones, it would save 2.4 million trees a year, according to Seventh Generation, a manufacturer of earth-friendly paper and cleaning products.

Stay away from paper products that use elemental chlorine bleach (or, chlorine gas) to whiten them: chlorine is carcinogenic. Totally chlorine free (TCF) napkins are the best—don't be put off by their brown color!—followed by processed chlorine free (PCF) and elemental chlorine free (ECF), if that's all that is available; these labels will appear on the packaging.

On average, each American uses twenty-two hundred napkins per year, which breaks down to six per day. If everyone used one napkin fewer a day, it would save billions of napkins from going into landfill. (Remember, paper napkins are not recyclable if they have food on them, although some urban areas do accept used napkins in their curbside composting programs.)

cork place-card holders
with seeded paper

Holiday celebrations often include uncorking a special bottle of wine or champagne, and the corks can do double duty by easily transforming into place-card holders for a dinner party. Cork is actually a very green material: biodegradable and renewable, it's made from the bark of the cork oak tree. The cork oak can live for hundreds of years, and when the bark has been stripped away, it grows back in nine years. The cork industry keeps these trees, and the wildlife that depends on them, alive. According to Portocork America, a manufacturer of natural cork closures, reforestation programs indicate that cork forests are growing at 4 percent a year, and more than 370,000 acres of cork forests have been planted in the Iberian Peninsula since 1988. The seeded paper for the place-cards can be planted in the spring.

- **Wine and champagne corks**

- **A sharp knife**

- **Scissors**

- **Seeded paper (see Resources) or recycled card paper from old Christmas or birthday cards**

- **Holiday rubber stamps**

- **Nontoxic ink pad**

- **Colored pens**

1. Place a cork on its side on a flat surface and carefully cut a slice into the top of the cork about ¼ inch/6.5 mm deep. Repeat with the remaining corks.

2. With the scissors, cut the card paper into rectangles 2½ inches/6 cm long by 1½ inches/4 cm high (or in Christmas shapes, if you prefer) and decorate with the holiday stamps.

3. With a colored pen, write the name of a guest on one side of a card and slide the card into the top of the cork. Arrange a place card at each table setting.

| ECO-INSPIRATION |

Besides using corks for craft projects (cork bulletin boards are easy and fun to make, as are cork trivets), you can send corks to organizations that reuse them (see Resources). Start a "green cork" campaign in your neighborhood by asking local restaurants and bars, as well as your neighbors, to collect corks for you to recycle.

pinecones with recycled glass

These cheerful pinecone decorations add life and color to both mantels and dining tables.

- Assorted pinecones
- Nontoxic silver and gold paint
- Small paintbrush
- Sheets of newspaper
- Nontoxic tacky glue
- Small pieces of different colored recycled glass (see Resources)

1. Paint the pinecones and let them dry on the newspaper.

2. Glue recycled glass pieces onto the pinecone points. Let dry.

3. Arrange the pinecones on a tabletop or mantel.

winter fruit and nut centerpieces

Having bowls of winter fruit and nuts as tabletop centerpieces reminds me of Christmas in Germany. These centerpieces are the ultimate green decoration. Buying seasonal fruit and nuts, using them for decoration, and then eating them subscribes to the concept of waste not, want not. If you decide to dry the fruit, the centerpiece can last for years and can ultimately wind up in your compost heap.

Use vintage bowls, trays, and serving dishes of different styles. I recently found a vintage Indian tray at an antique shop and filled it with walnuts and dried pomegranates: so simple and so pretty. Add little glass votive candles for a perfectly Elizabethan Christmas dinner.

For fruit, use fresh or dried pomegranates, fresh persimmons, mandarins, oranges, lemons, or satsumas. For nuts, try walnuts, almonds, or hazelnuts in their shells. Keep a nutcracker nearby; you will notice your guests snacking on the centerpieces throughout the meal.

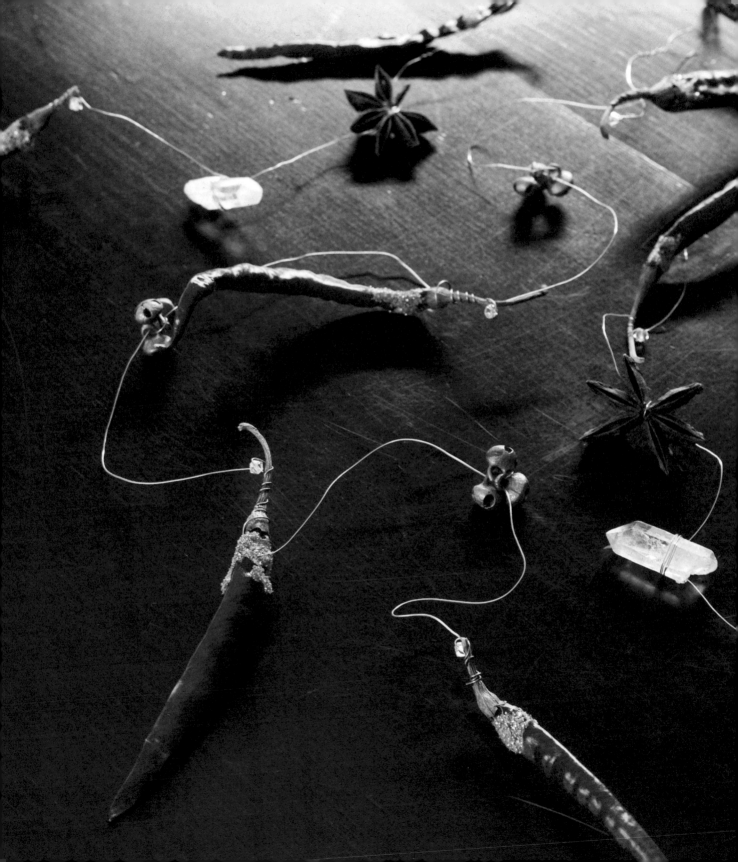

wire table decorations: chile and quartz crystal

These charming table decorations add simple flair to your dining table. Create a centerpiece by curling them up and placing candles among them, or lay them across the table. The chiles add a New Mexican touch, while the crystals bring nature to your table.

GATHER

- About 8 small dried red chiles
- Small paintbrush
- Nontoxic white glue
- Nontoxic silver glitter
- 8 feet/244 cm of 26-gauge silver wire
- 4 small quartz crystals about 1½ inches/4 cm long (available online or at craft shops; see Resources)
- Wire cutters

CREATE

1. Paint the top of each chile with glue, sprinkle with glitter, and let dry.

2. Take one end of the wire and wrap it tightly around the stem of one chile several times.

3. Place a quartz crystal 1 to 2 inches/ 2.5 to 5 cm down the wire from the last chili and tightly wrap the wire around the top of the crystal six or seven times. Then twist both ends of the wire around the back of the crystal to secure it. (You also can use a drop of glue to secure the crystal.) Repeat with remaining chilis and crystals.

4. Cut away any excess wire with the wire cutters.

wire table decorations: chile and bell

This is a variation on the Wire Table Decorations (see page 63) using festive bells.

GATHER

CREATE

- About 8 small dried red chiles

- Small paintbrush

- Nontoxic white glue

- Nontoxic gold glitter

- 24 small bells

- 8 feet/244 cm of 20-gauge gold wire

- Wire cutters

1. Paint the top of each chile with glue, sprinkle with glitter, and let dry.

2. Take one end of the wire and wrap it tightly around the stem of a chile several times.

3. String three bells closely together, 1 to 2 inches/2.5 to 5 cm down the wire. Tightly twist both ends of the wire around the back side of bells to secure in place. Repeat seven times alternating chile and bells.

4. Cut away any excess wire with the wire cutters.

CELEBRITY GREEN TIP

LAUREN BUSH, *creator of the FEED bag*
www.FEEDprojects.org

It is so "eco" and fun to be a little more creative with holiday decorations, instead of just going the store bought route. The key is to utilize things you already own to create a more personal and unique holiday atmosphere. For example, my boyfriend, David, and I threw a Holiday Fiesta party one year, using these bright Mexican blankets we already owned as the main decor. Also, some hand-cut snowflakes or homade ornaments really tops off any room!

glittered dried rose petals

A rose is a rose is a rose. Choose brightly colored roses like red, fuchsia, or pink for these decorations, which can be used time and time again. Organicbouquet.com is the only online resource I know of that sells organic and fair-trade roses. After drying the roses, you can sprinkle them with a Christmassy essential oil, such as cinnamon, clove, or nutmeg. Scatter the dried petals on the dining table or the mantel, or place them in vintage glass or silver-colored bowls around the house. It will be as if Christmas fairies flew around the house, leaving behind little surprises.

GATHER

CREATE

- **Rose petals (see Note)**
- **Tissue paper or wire screen**
- **Nontoxic glue**
- **Nontoxic glitter**

1. Spread the rose petals in a single layer on the tissue paper or wire screen and place them where there will be plenty of ventilation. (But don't put them in direct sunlight.) Drying will take several days, depending on the rose variety and its moisture content.

2. When the petals are dry, place glue on the edges of some petals and sprinkle with the glitter. Allow them to dry overnight, then sprinkle them around the dinner table.

3. Alternatively, sprinkle fresh rose petals on the holiday table and skip the glitter. (These can then be added to your compost pile.)

NOTE: *If fresh rose petals are not available, do a search on Ebay for fabric flower petals and glitter. They will last for years.*

parting gifts

Guests are always grateful when you open your doors to them and share your hospitality during the holidays. To add one more special touch, offer them a parting gift as they leave the warmth of your home. It can be a simple piece of organic fair-trade chocolate, a homemade glitter-shell candle, or a little pot of rosemary that they can replant. Even a small token will show your gratitude for their friendship this season. Rather than handing out parting gifts at the end of the evening, make them work double duty by placing them on the table and using them as table decorations during the celebration. The following three ideas—Mini Rosemary Pots, Mini Glitter-Shell Tea Light Candles, and Decorated Matchboxes—all send a thoughtful message to your guests.

mini rosemary pots

Head to your local nursery and purchase some small rosemary plants. Place them in small aluminum pots or cans and tie a festive used ribbon around them.

EXPERT GREEN TIP

JENNY HWA, *founder and designer, Loyale Clothing*

www.loyaleclothing.com

One of my new eco-Christmas traditions is to see just how sustainably my staff and I can dress for all of our holiday festivities. Not many people know that buying organic clothing is just as important as buying organic food; it takes nearly a pound of chemical fertilizers and pesticides to produce the cotton for one outfit of conventional jeans and a T-shirt. That is two cups of synthetic chemicals for just one outfit, and those chemicals remain in the fibers indefinitely and end up on your skin. So consider wearing gorgeously green organic-cotton clothing to all your holiday parties—and giving it as gifts, too!

mini glitter-shell tea light candles

These magical little tea lights are fun and easy to make. Not only do they make great parting gifts, they also look wonderful when lit all around the house. I like to use clamshells, but you can use any seashells that you've found on the beach.

GATHER

CREATE

- 1 to 1½ pounds/450 to 675 g coconut wax or beeswax (any nontoxic wax will work; see Note)

- An old cooking pan

- 10 small to medium-size shells

- Sheets of newspaper

- Aromatherapy fragrance or essential oils, such as clove or cinnamon

- Candy thermometer

- Small metal funnel

- Zinc or tin nontoxic pretabbed wicks (see Resources)

- Scissors

- Fine nontoxic silver glitter

1. Place the wax in the pan over medium heat and melt it completely. While the wax is melting, arrange the shells on a layer of newspaper.

2. When the wax has melted, remove from heat, add 3 to 4 drops of the fragrance oil, and stir.

3. Return the pot of wax to the heat and bring it to the proper pouring temperature, about 175°F/80°C. Using the funnel, pour the hot wax into each shell; fill the shell to the lip, but be careful not to let it overflow. Make one candle as a test before filling remaining shells just to get a sense of how the wax pours.

4. Wait for the wax to cool, about 4 to 5 minutes. You will notice the wax becomes more opaque. While the wax is cooling, prepare the wicks by straightening them and cutting them to 1 to 1½ inches/2.5 to 4 cm long.

5. Insert the wicks into the wax till the tab sticks to the bottom; be sure to position the wick in the center of the shell. You do not want more than ⅓ to ¼ inch/ 8.5 to 6.5 mm of the wick sticking out of the wax, although you can trim the wicks again later if necessary. If the wick starts to tilt and pull the wick off center, lightly bend the wick back to straighten it. Make sure to add the wick before the wax solidifies.

6. Sprinkle a small amount of glitter onto the surface of each candle.

7. To avoid any bubbling or cracking, allow the candles to sit and dry fully before moving them (3 to 4 hours). Once the candles are completely dry, trim the wicks down to the desired length (for a longer burn time, trim wicks to ¼ inch / 6.5 mm.

NOTE: *If you have any leftover wax, pour it into glasses with half-burned votive candles.*

DO RIGHT BY CANDLELIGHT

Turning off the lights and enjoying candlelight is romantic and soothing. Candles can create a beautiful glow in any setting. Although candlelight is eco-friendly (you use less electricity), not all candles are.

Most candles on the market are made from paraffin, a petroleum-based material, and contain dyes, artificial fragrances, and synthetic wicks that contain lead. (Lead is banned in many countries, but it's still used widely in Asia and South America, which export many candles.) Commercial candles also emit toxins such as benzene and toluene (which the EPA has declared are carcinogens), in addition to petro-carbon soot, which over time can build up on walls, drapes, and furniture.

All-natural candles made from beeswax, soy, or palm wax, with nontoxic cotton wicks, are the greenest choice. They are biodegradable, they burn clean, and they burn longer than conventional candles. Candle manufacturers are not required to list the candle ingredients on the packaging, so if it doesn't say it's all-natural, it's most likely not. (To get a full list of ingredients, call the manufacturer directly.)

Beeswax candles burn three times longer than soy and paraffin candles, and they give off a lovely honey scent; just be sure the label says 100 percent beeswax: some candles are beeswax-paraffin blends. Soy candles are made from soybean oil, and they burn cool (about 106 degrees Fahrenheit/41 degrees Celsius), so they won't seriously burn anyone who accidentally touches them, an important feature if you have children around. However, more than 75 percent of soy grown in the United States is genetically modified, so ask the companies whether they use GMO soy for their candles. Palm wax is made from palm oil, extracted from the fruit of the palm tree. Because palm wax candles are sturdier than soy candles, they make the best pillar candles.

Scented candles produce much more soot than unscented ones, but if you can't live without scented candles, make sure they are made with natural essential oils instead of synthetic fragrances.

Finally, before you buy that pretty set of candles, think about how they are packaged; buy a boxed set rather than ones individually wrapped in plastic. One last tip: to reduce soot buildup, keep wicks trimmed to ¼ inch/6.5 mm.

decorated matchboxes

My husband and I collect matchboxes from places all over the world. For this craft, use matchboxes you have collected through the years, or purchase sustainably made ones. They make a perfect parting gift on their own or paired with a Mini Glitter-Shell Tea Light Candle (see page 67).

GATHER

- Assorted matchboxes
- Nontoxic glue
- Scraps of wrapping paper or tissue paper
- Sequins, bits of ribbon, tiny seashells, or other found items

CREATE

Place a bit of glue on one side of the matchbox and decorate with paper, sequins, ribbon, or other items. Be careful not to let the glue drip onto the edges of the box where you strike the matches. Let dry completely.

| TABLE DECORATIONS |

I love to go to the flea market at Christmastime to pick up vintage decorations. You can find imitation studded fruit, large glass colored balls, and other Christmas decorations that are perfect for decorating your tabletop for a holiday dinner party. And the best part is, you're reusing someone else's treasures. I have started a vintage charger-plate collection based on my flea-market finds. Each one is different from the next, and it's fun to use them for dinner parties. Using vintage tableware is a personal choice, though. Some people worry about whether these items are safe, citing, for example, lead content in old crystal (this is now government regulated). If you're buying anything you will be eating from, you'll want to be careful. But I buy vintage tableware all the time.

stuffed mushrooms

One of my favorite things about parties are the appetizers. I love tasting all the different flavors in small bites. I'm particularly fond of stuffed mushrooms: woodsy, garlicky, cheesy, and baked to perfection. The only problem is, I can eat twenty of them in a row, so I have to keep passing that tray.

| MAKES 12 MUSHROOMS |

- 12 cremini mushrooms
- 1 medium shiitake mushroom, with stem, roughly chopped
- 1 tablespoon olive oil
- ¼ small yellow onion, finely chopped
- ½ teaspoon fresh thyme
- ½ teaspoon soy sauce
- Salt and pepper to taste
- 2 tablespoons bread crumbs
- 1 tablespoon finely grated Parmesan cheese
- 1 teaspoon minced fresh flat-leaf parsley
- ½ tablespoon unsalted butter
- 2 tablespoons water

1. Preheat the oven to 350°F/180°C (Gas Mark 4).

2. Remove the stems from the cremini mushrooms by popping them out. Set aside the caps. Place the stems in a food processor with the shiitake mushroom and pulse until the mushrooms are minced. Be sure not to over-pulse, because the mushrooms can turn to mush fairly quickly. Set aside.

3. Heat the olive oil in a medium pan over medium-low heat and add the onion. Sauté until the onion is translucent, 3 to 4 minutes.

4. Add the thyme and minced mushroom stems and sauté for 3 minutes. Stir in the soy sauce and season with salt and pepper. Stir in 1 tablespoon bread crumbs. Remove from heat, transfer to a medium-size bowl, and let cool for 5 minutes. Stir in the Parmesan.

5. Stuff each mushroom cap with a spoonful of mushroom mixture until each one is nicely rounded.

6. In a small bowl, combine the parsley and remaining bread crumbs. Heat the butter in a small pan over medium heat and sauté the parsley mixture until browned, 5 to 6 minutes.

7. Sprinkle each stuffed mushroom cap with a pinch of the parsley mixture.

8. Place the mushroom caps in a small baking dish and add the water to the dish. Bake for 20 minutes. Serve warm or at room temperature.

EXPERT GREEN TIP

MATT PETERSON, CEO, *Global Green*
www.globalgreen.org

Many heartwarming thoughts come to mind when I think of my child-hood Christmases. The most inspirational are from the couple of years when my family struggled a bit, during the recession in the late 1970s. We decided to be creative with our Christmas gifts and means of celebrating. My sister, brother, mom, dad, and I each made clove-studded oranges—otherwise known as pomander balls, which in the fifteenth century were used to scent closets and drawers—and I made colorful drawings for each of my family members. These simple acts of love reminded me of the true nature of the Christmas holiday.

As I reflect on this, I'm also reminded of Bill McKibben's book *Hundred-Dollar Holiday: The Case for a More Joyful Holiday*. Bill, one of my true heroes, makes an impassioned plea for a less consumer-oriented, more meaningful holiday, and he challenges each of us to spend no more than a hundred dollars on all gifts. As he says, the idea was an effort to counter the "relentless onslaught of commercials and catalogs that try to say Christmas is only Christmas if it comes from a store." I agree that we should return to a simpler sort of Christmas celebration and remember what it's really about: the joy and reverence for life as embodied in our family, friends, and togetherness.

gorgonzola and grape toasts

This hors d'oeuvre is not for the faint of heart. Gorgonzola dolce has a lovely, distinct nutty flavor that combines perfectly with the grapes of the season; but while it is sweeter and softer than most Gorgonzolas, it still has the boldness of a blue cheese. This is my mother's recipe; she recommends serving red wine with these delightful toasts. Be sure to pass them around while they're still warm.

| MAKES 20 TOASTS |

- ½ baguette, sliced into ⅓-inch/ 8.5-mm rounds (about 20 slices)
- 2 to 3 tablespoons olive oil
- Salt and pepper to taste
- ½ cup/100 g red grapes, sliced lengthwise
- 4 to 5 ounces/110 to 140 g Gorgonzola dolce, at room temperature
- 1 teaspoon minced fresh thyme

1. Preheat the oven to 375°F/190°C (Gas Mark 5).

2. Arrange the baguette rounds on a large baking sheet.

3. Pour the olive oil into a small bowl. Using a pastry brush, lightly brush each bread piece with the oil. Sprinkle each slice with salt and pepper.

4. Bake for 10 to 12 minutes. Let cool.

5. Lower the oven temperature to 300°F/ 150°C (Gas Mark 2).

6. In a medium bowl, mix the grapes and Gorgonzola until well combined. Add the thyme, season with salt and pepper, and mix well.

7. Spread the Gorgonzola mixture evenly onto each bread slice and bake for 3 to 5 minutes. Serve warm.

GLOBAL GREEN:

Christmas in Canada

Going green comes naturally to Canadians, where living Christmas trees decorate most homes and local food is served for Christmas dinner. (In British Columbia, fresh or smoked salmon is the prized dish.) The Environmental Choice Eco-Label is a national eco-certification program that recognizes products that are less harmful to the environment, so it's easy to shop for products that are earth-friendly.

artichoke dip with baked pita chips

This rich, comforting dip is perfect for winter weather and utilizes the delicious flavor of canned or jarred artichoke hearts.

| SERVES 6 TO 8 |

FOR THE ARTICHOKE DIP

- 16-ounce/455-g can artichoke hearts
- ½ cup/110 g mayonnaise
- 1¼ cups/10 oz. sour cream
- ¼ cup/7 g plus 2 tablespoons grated Parmesan cheese
- 1 clove garlic (to be placed whole in the food processor)
- Salt and white pepper to taste
- Juice of ½ lemon

FOR THE PITA CHIPS

- 6 pieces pita bread
- ¾ cup/180 ml olive oil
- 2 teaspoons paprika
- 1 teaspoon ground cumin
- 1 teaspoon ground coriander
- 1½ teaspoons garlic powder
- 1 tablespoon minced fresh flat-leaf parsley
- Salt and pepper to taste

TO MAKE THE ARTICHOKE DIP:

Combine all ingredients in the bowl of a food processor and puree until smooth. Refrigerate until ready to serve.

TO MAKE THE PITA CHIPS:

1. Preheat the oven to 400°F/200°C (Gas Mark 6).

2. Cut the pita rounds into six triangular pieces, then cut each piece in half.

3. In a medium bowl, combine the olive oil, paprika, cumin, coriander, garlic powder, and parsley. Season with salt and pepper. Add the pita pieces and, using your hands, mix until the pita bread is well coated.

4. Place the pita pieces in a single layer on a large baking sheet. Bake for 6 to 7 minutes on the middle rack of the oven, until lightly browned.

5. Remove the baking sheet from the oven, turn the pita pieces over, and bake for another 6 to 7 minutes, or until golden and crispy. (Check them frequently to be sure they're not burning.)

6. Serve on a platter with the artichoke dip.

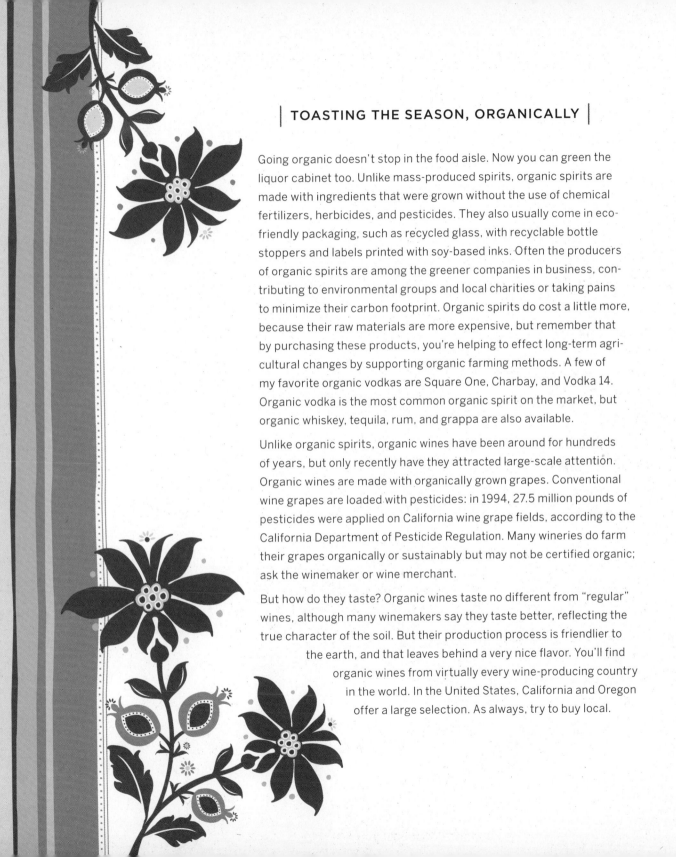

TOASTING THE SEASON, ORGANICALLY

Going organic doesn't stop in the food aisle. Now you can green the liquor cabinet too. Unlike mass-produced spirits, organic spirits are made with ingredients that were grown without the use of chemical fertilizers, herbicides, and pesticides. They also usually come in eco-friendly packaging, such as recycled glass, with recyclable bottle stoppers and labels printed with soy-based inks. Often the producers of organic spirits are among the greener companies in business, contributing to environmental groups and local charities or taking pains to minimize their carbon footprint. Organic spirits do cost a little more, because their raw materials are more expensive, but remember that by purchasing these products, you're helping to effect long-term agricultural changes by supporting organic farming methods. A few of my favorite organic vodkas are Square One, Charbay, and Vodka 14. Organic vodka is the most common organic spirit on the market, but organic whiskey, tequila, rum, and grappa are also available.

Unlike organic spirits, organic wines have been around for hundreds of years, but only recently have they attracted large-scale attention. Organic wines are made with organically grown grapes. Conventional wine grapes are loaded with pesticides: in 1994, 27.5 million pounds of pesticides were applied on California wine grape fields, according to the California Department of Pesticide Regulation. Many wineries do farm their grapes organically or sustainably but may not be certified organic; ask the winemaker or wine merchant.

But how do they taste? Organic wines taste no different from "regular" wines, although many winemakers say they taste better, reflecting the true character of the soil. But their production process is friendlier to the earth, and that leaves behind a very nice flavor. You'll find organic wines from virtually every wine-producing country in the world. In the United States, California and Oregon offer a large selection. As always, try to buy local.

prosciutto and
goat cheese–wrapped figs

Figs are at their peak during the holiday season. I love drizzling chestnut honey over these tasty gems before baking, but feel free to use any honey you have on hand. Purple figs are my personal favorite, but green ones will work perfectly, too. These will disappear quickly!

| SERVES 6 TO 8 |

- 8 fresh figs cut in half horizontally
- 3 ounces/90 g soft goat's milk cheese
- 8 thin slices prosciutto, cut in half lengthwise
- Chestnut honey
- Olive oil
- Salt and freshly cracked pepper to taste
- Ground cinnamon for garnish

1. Preheat the oven to 375°F/190°C (Gas Mark 5).

2. Place a small dab of goat's milk cheese onto the cut side of a fig. Tightly wrap the fig half with one piece of prosciutto and place it on a baking sheet. Repeat with remaining figs and prosciutto.

3. Drizzle honey over the fig pieces, then drizzle with olive oil. Top with salt and freshly cracked pepper.

4. Bake the figs for 5 to 6 minutes. Serve warm, arranged on a platter and garnished with a sprinkle of cinnamon.

| SUSTAINABLE SERVING IDEAS |

When hosting guests, use glass cups, your own dishes, and silverware instead of plastic. If the prospect of cleaning all these dishes is too daunting or you don't have enough to go around, look for disposable bamboo or non-GMO compostable plates instead of plastic. Bambu brand plates are recyclable and biodegradable, and Whole Foods' 365 brand plates are made from sugarcane and reed pulp—fast-growing renewable resources—and are compostable. If plastic is your only option, choose wisely: Preserve brand recycled plastic tableware and silverware is dishwasher-safe and can be reused and recycled. If you can't find that particular brand, just look for plastic ware with the no. 5 recycling symbol, which indicates that it was made from polypropylene and has a low resin density.

If you entertain often (and have enough storage space), it's much better to buy a set of dishes that you can use for every party. They'll last for years, and you can lend the dishes out to friends for their parties. Some stores, such as Crate & Barrel, even carry recycled glassware. The next best thing is to rent dishes, silverware, glasses, and linens. (Renting isn't the top choice, because rental companies use so much toxic bleach and hot water to clean the rental items.)

pomegranate antioxidant cocktail

Ruby red pomegranates have quite a history. In Buddhism they're considered a blessed fruit. Muhammad believed that pomegranates would bring both emotional and physical peace because of their nutrients. Pomegranates are high in antioxidants, which are free-radical-fighting powerhouses. Their season runs from October through January, so enjoy them while they last. I use Veev in this cocktail, a liqueur made from the South American açaí berry, another fruit high in antioxidants, but feel free to substitute vodka.

| SERVES 1 |

- 3 tablespoons Veev
- ½ cup/125 ml sweetened pomegranate juice
- 2 tablespoons fresh lime juice
- ¼ to ½ cup crushed ice
- 10 fresh pomegranate seeds, for garnish
- 1 lime wedge, for garnish

1. In a cocktail mixer, mix together the Veev, pomegranate juice, lime juice, and ice.

2. Place the pomegranate seeds in a 4- to 6-ounce cocktail glass. Pour the pomegranate mixture into the glass and garnish with the lime wedge.

GLOBAL GREEN:

Christmas in Sweden

In Sweden, the Christmas season lasts almost two months. Windows are usually decorated with candles and hyacinth, and people often build snow caves, called *snölyktor*, and put candles inside to illuminate them. Christmas tree decorations take advantage of natural resources: animal ornaments made of straw, cardboard angels and stars, glass ornaments. The Swedes also decorate their trees with edible items such as dried fruit and berries, nuts, and chocolate, which they eat on Christmas Eve. You could borrow that idea and eat the edibles on your tree on the night of your holiday party with your friends and family.

Traditionally, no guest is allowed to leave a Swedish home without eating or drinking something, for fear that the Christmas spirit will leave with them. What better excuse to indulge your friends and family with delicious holiday treats?

SUSTAINABLE CELEBRATING:
| CHAMPAGNE AND CAVIAR |

Champagne and caviar are a holiday indulgence for many, but before you plan this special meal, consider the environmental impact of these luxuries. Caviar is salted fish roe, the most prized coming from sturgeon. Wild sturgeon have been extremely overfished, leading the United States to ban imported beluga caviar in 2005 (the ban has since been lifted). A much greener option is domestically harvested caviar from farmed sturgeon and paddlefish. Tsar Nicoulai, a California caviar producer, is my favorite source for sustainable caviar (see Resources). Tsar Nicoulai's new sturgeon farm in Wilton, California, is designed on the principles of organic food production, which require the fostering of biodiversity, biological cycles, and biological activity in an integrated system that is ecologically sustainable. In the past ten years, Americans purchased 130,000 pounds of imported caviar each year, so our buying power will make a difference in pushing for more sustainable sources of caviar. Be sure to check the practices and processes of any caviar advertised as "sustainable." I have mentioned Tsar Nicoulai because this is the only U.S. company that maintains a sound sustainable system.

Uncorking a bottle of champagne is a planet-friendly way to celebrate the season if you choose an organic bottle. Some wonderful organic French champagne producers include Serge Mathieu, Jean-Pierre Fleury, and Philipponnat. In addition, the champagne industry as a whole is starting to think green: in 2003, the Comité Interprofessionel du Vin de Champagne (CIVC, the French champagne producers' association) conducted an environmental survey and set guidelines for producers to reduce their carbon dioxide emissions. For those of us in the United States, the main environmental concern is shipping, since the bottles of organic bubbly come from Europe. If possible, select a locally made sparkling wine instead of champagne; California, Oregon, Washington, New Mexico, and New York all produce delicious sparkling wines. And don't forget to save the corks for Cork Place-Card Holders (page 59).

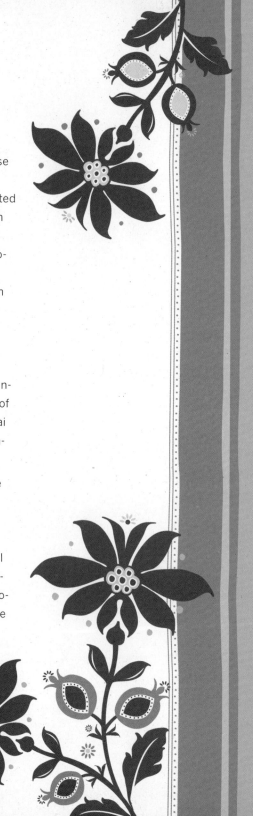

BREAK THE PLASTIC BOTTLE HABIT

With friends and family in town, it's tempting to stock the refrigerator with bottled water, but those containers are far from earth-friendly. Plastic water bottles are an environmental disaster, because petroleum is used to make them and the recycling rates are low (according the Container Recycling Institute, 86 percent of plastic bottles nationwide are not recycled). In California alone, three million water bottles end up in the trash each day, according to a 2003 report by the California Department of Conservation. The report showed that only 16 percent of polyethylene terephthalate water bottles (that is, no. 1 plastic bottles, or PET) sold in California are being recycled. At that rate, the amount of water bottles thrown in the trash in 2013 would be enough to create a two-lane, six-inch/15-cm-deep highway that stretches along the entire coast of California. When the bottles end up in the trash, they're either incinerated, which releases greenhouse gases, or landfilled, where they take as long as a thousand years to degrade. Glass bottles aren't much better; a lot of fuel is burned trucking those heavy glass bottles to your local retailer. What's more, bottled water can cost up to ten thousand times more per gallon than tap water.

There is one good thing to say about PET water bottles: when they are recycled, they can be turned into many other materials, such as outerwear, rugs, and even backpacks. The plastic is melted and pressed into long fibers, which are spun into yarn and then woven together. In 1993, Patagonia became the first company to use polyester fleece made from plastic bottles. Every 150 fleece jackets saves a barrel of oil and prevents about half a ton of air pollution, according to Patagonia, and in the past thirteen years, the company has saved 86 million plastic bottles from the landfill.

A few tips for greener beverages:

- For dinner and cocktail parties, serve pitchers of filtered water instead of bottled water. I got inspired by a recent trip to Italy, where many of my friends refill used wine bottles with water. The bottles look great on the dinner table.

- Choose aluminum cans whenever possible; they are the greenest packaging available. Lighter than glass, cans require less fuel when shipped and are more likely than glass to be recycled. (This last point is still debated among environmentalists, but for now, aluminum wins out over glass.) Glass is the next-best choice, but skip the plastic.

- Milk sold in glass bottles is preferable to that sold in cartons, which usually aren't recyclable because of their wax lining. Milk cartons are compostable in some curbside composting programs, however; check to see if your community has such a program.

- Buy local: beer from a local brewer (if you're having a big party, buy a keg, which is reusable), teas, and other locally made nonalcoholic drinks.

- Brew your own tea, or make lemonade and juice spritzers at home, saving money and natural resources.

trimming

Decorating a Christmas tree is one of the best things about the holidays. It's also a tradition that raises many questions about the most environmentally friendly way to **deck the halls**. As important as your trimmings are, deciding what sort of tree you'll decorate will have more impact than almost any other decision you can make. In this chapter, I'll share my and some experts' opinions on the real vs. fake debate—it's a hotly contested question, and there are advantages to both.

Once you've decided on the tree, it's time to trim. Making **ornaments** has become a favorite holiday activity for my family—my daughter and I love making Salt Dough Ornaments (page 91). It's a great opportunity to **bond** with your child, and hanging these handmade ornaments year after year makes lasting memories. In fact I still have the walnut ornaments my mom made when I was a child.

Make trimming your tree about connecting with **nature** and taking the time to go outside and create treasures from natural resources. Skip the plastic ornaments and tinsel and think of more natural decorations, such as nuts, fruit, twigs, leaves, and paper. Also hunt around the house for materials you already have: glass balls, colorful ribbons, and twinkling lights (LED, of course) also bring joy to a room.

Invite **friends** or family over, share a meal, and spend time hanging ornaments. A few simple recipes are all you'll need to feed your guests; my favorite is a big bowl of Parmesan and Yeast Flake Popcorn (page 112).

REAL VS. FAKE:
THE GREAT CHRISTMAS TREE DEBATE

This is an evergreen topic for environmentalists come December. Although there are arguments for both real trees and fake trees, I stand firmly in favor of the real thing. An artificial tree has an average lifespan of four years in your home, then sits indefinitely in a landfill. Most plastic trees are made with polyvinyl chloride (PVC), the least recyclable plastic; even worse, it requires lead in its manufacturing process. So making artificial trees emits dangerous carcinogens that affect both the planet and the workers who manufacture the trees. Unless you have a vintage artificial tree made of paper, which is the greenest tree choice, a real tree is best.

In the United States, 98 percent of Christmas trees are grown sustainably on farms, and each acre of Christmas trees averages enough daily oxygen production for eighteen people. But according to the Sierra Club, many holiday trees are doused with pesticides and artificial colorings. These pesticides may end up in the water supply while the tree is growing and again when it's discarded. So if you've decided to go with a cut tree, make it an organically grown one (see Resources).

A living tree is the best choice; it arrives potted, and then after the holidays you plant it in your backyard or in a park. In some forests you can cut your own, which helps thin dense forests and prevent wildfires. See Resources for more information about buying a living tree or securing the necessary permits to cut your own tree. No matter what type of real tree you buy, go online and plant five more (see Resources).

Of course, the greenest choice of all is skipping the tree altogether. Decorating the trees or shrubs outside your house with LED lights, recycled-paper snowflakes, or vintage Christmas decorations is still festive and cheerful.

If you buy a cut tree, be sure to dispose of it properly. Each year, ten million of the thirty-three million Christmas trees sold in North America end up in a landfill. Instead of trashing it, recycle your tree or, better yet, compost or mulch it (the greenest option). Some cities offer tree recycling programs, but you also can go to www.earth911.org to find a tree recycling program near you. If you can, chop the tree into firewood.

CHRISTOPHER GAVIGAN, author and CEO of *Healthy Child, Healthy World*
www.healthychild.org

In my childhood memories, the holidays are a glorious time of giving, eggnog, and itchy turtle-neck sweaters. It was my grandmother who loved the "natural tree" and imparted the respect for live trees, which we'd plant in our thawed yards come early spring in Connecticut. My brothers and I could travel the yard over the years, point to a tree, and recall its first year and associated (notorious) stories. The special part was that we'd deck the halls with real holly and evergreen wreaths—none of the artificial decorations that are typically made of cheap PVC plastic (read: *lead hazard*—children and family beware). And specific to the tree, we'd string popcorn, seasonal berries (typically cranberries), colored dough, and cinnamon sticks—organic, of course. Our little hands would be pricked a few times, but our long strings of garland were draped across the trees with special care and added the perfect touch and homemade cheer. The birds, squirrels, and deer thanked us as we placed the garlands outside on low-lying branches to feed their winter bellies. It's a simple, healthful, biodegradable, special, and fun family tradition I'll always remember and continue to follow.

GLOBAL GREEN:

CHRISTMAS IN AUSTRALIA

Australians celebrate the holiday in their own green way, and there are some wonderful ideas to borrow. Because Christmas falls at the beginning of summer, the traditional Christmas meal centers around cold salads and meats and grilled seafood, celebrating the warm weather. Christmas trees decorate the streets and homes, but Australians also display native plants and flowers that bloom in red and green, such as Christmas bush and Christmas bells. I love that so many Australians head to the beach on Christmas (Bondi Beach, in Sydney, gets more than forty thousand visitors on Christmas Day), embracing the natural beauty of the country and spending time together.

super-easy tree skirt

I am always at a loss when it comes to a tree skirt. I usually take an old sheet or piece of inherited vintage fabric, wrap it loosely around the tree trunk, and make do. This tree skirt won't require much more effort than that, but it looks a lot more polished. Simply take an old round tablecloth, preferably in Christmas colors. (You often can find old Christmas tablecloths at secondhand stores.) With sharp scissors, slice a slit from the edge to the center. At the center, cut a hole large enough to accommodate the base of the tree trunk or container. You can either attach snaps or Velcro to hold the slit closed, or just leave it free and layer one side over the other. If you want to go the extra mile, sew pieces of lace, buttons, or glass beads around the hem.

EXPERT GREEN TIP

MARY CORDARO, *environmental consultant and creator of the Mary Cordaro Collection of Organic Beds and Bedding*

http://h3environmental.com

For the past twenty years, my family has followed the centuries-old tradition of putting candles on the tree. Doing without electric lights on the tree puts one in a totally different frame of mind at Christmas. It literally takes the charge out of it. Turning off all the lights in the house for about an hour and watching dozens of pure beeswax candles emit their soft glow puts everyone in a peaceful, happy, and grateful state of mind.

salt dough ornaments

This is an excellent craft to do with children. When I first made these with my daughter, she kept asking me if we would eat them once they were finished baking. I told her we could, but they would be really salty. They are definitely not for eating, but they look adorable hanging from tree branches or anywhere around the house.

|MAKES 30 TO 40 ORNAMENTS, DEPENDING ON THE SIZE COOKIE CUTTERS YOU USE|

GATHER

- 2 cups/250 g all-purpose flour, plus extra for rolling the dough
- 1 cup/200 g salt
- 1 cup/250 ml water
- Rolling pin
- Cookie cutters (various shapes and sizes)
- Cookie sheet
- Toothpick
- Used yarn or ribbon, cut in 3- to 4-inch/8- to 10-cm lengths
- Nontoxic glue (optional)
- Nontoxic gold and silver glitter (optional)

CREATE

1. Preheat the oven to 250°F/120°C.

2. In a medium bowl, whisk together the flour and salt. Add the water and stir until the dough is well blended and no traces of flour remain.

3. Knead the dough on a flat surface until smooth, about 8 to 10 minutes. Do not let the dough get too rubbery.

4. On a floured surface, use the rolling pin to roll out the dough until it's about ¼ inch/6.5 mm thick. With the cookie cutters, cut out shapes and place them on the (ungreased) cookie sheet. Use the toothpick to make a hole at the top of each ornament large enough for the yarn or ribbon to fit through, and bake for 2 hours.

5. When the ornaments are done baking, let them cool, slip a piece of yarn or ribbon through each hole, and knot.

6. If you like, draw glue designs on the ornaments and then cover them with glitter. Allow them to dry, then shake off the excess glitter.

lightbulb ornaments

Don't throw those used lightbulbs out. Reuse them by assigning them a new purpose as Christmas tree decorations. Always be sure to handle and store them properly. For this craft, avoid compact fluorescent lightbulbs: they contain mercury, and if you break them accidentally, you could be exposed to harmful mercury vapor.

GATHER

- **Used ribbon, yarn, or any type of craft string**
- **Scissors**
- **Old lightbulbs (any shape or size)**
- **Small paintbrushes**
- **Paint in Christmas colors (nontoxic but permanent)**

CREATE

1. Cut the ribbon or yarn in 5- to 6-inch/ 13- to 15-cm lengths.

2. Tie a length of ribbon or yarn around the base of each lightbulb.

3. Paint the lightbulbs and let them dry by hanging them from a light fixture or on a shower-curtain rod.

4. Tie the bulbs to the branches of your tree, or tie the ribbon or yarn into a loop and hang the bulbs over the branches.

CELEBRITY GREEN TIP

| AMY SMART, ACTOR |

After Christmas, my family and I used to remove the pine needles from the Christmas tree and make drawer sachets with used fabric, such as old pillowcases. The sachets made our linens and undergarments smell like Christmas for months.

GLOBAL GREEN:

| CHRISTMAS IN GERMANY |

Germany comes alive at Christmastime, with the holiday festivities running from December 1 through January 6. The Germans were the first to use Christmas trees for decoration, and the first ornaments were candles. Glass ornaments, nuts, fruit, and other edible adornments soon followed, but tradition dictates that the tree isn't trimmed until December 24—and then only the adults are involved, preparing the tree and house for the children. When my brother and I were children, we would lurk in the hall, full of anticipation, waiting for the adults to finish decorating the tree. December 25 is a day for relaxing and spending time with family. When the tree is taken down on January 6, the children get to eat the edible decorations.

vintage chinese egg ornaments

Egg decorations are usually made at Easter time, but I love decorating my tree with these egg ornaments. You can use paper with holiday designs, but I love using Chinese newspaper and adding gold paint. Handle the eggs carefully while making the ornaments and storing them; the eggs are fragile, but properly stored, they will last for years.

GATHER

CREATE

- Pieces of used tissue paper, newspaper, holiday wrapping paper, Chinese or Japanese (or other language) newspaper

- Scissors

- 12 eggs

- Sterilized needle (see Note)

- 2 small bowls

- Gold paint (nontoxic but permanent)

- Paintbrushes

- White glue

- Water

- Gold, silver, or other colored thread (you also can use fishing line, if you have some)

1. Cut the paper into strips about ½ inch/ 1.25 cm wide and 2 inches/5 cm long.

2. Using the needle, carefully make a hole in each end of an egg. The holes should be larger than a pinprick, about 1 centimeter in diameter—just large enough to blow out the egg whites—and the bottom hole should be slightly larger than the top hole. Put one end of the egg against your mouth and blow the egg whites and yolk into a bowl (use them for eggnog or for baking). Repeat for each egg.

3. Paint the eggs gold and let dry. (The gold will eventually show through the paper, but feel free to skip the paint; the eggs look just as lovely covered only in paper.)

4. Take a strip of paper and cover one side with glue. Wrap the strip around the painted egg and gently smooth the edges down. Repeat until the egg is completely covered with paper strips. Repeat with remaining eggs.

5. In a small bowl, mix a small amount of glue with a drop or two of water. With a paintbrush, paint over the papered eggs to seal the paper.

6. With the needle, repuncture the hole through the glued paper at the top of the egg. Then allow the egg to dry for several hours.

7. Cut a 6- to 7-inch/15- to 17-cm length of thread, fold it in half, and knot each end of the thread. (The knots should be small enough to fit both of them through the top hole.) Using the needle, push both knotted ends through the top hole of the egg. Place two drops of glue over the hole and let dry. Repeat with remaining eggs.

NOTE: *Sterilize the needle by holding it over a flame for 10 seconds.*

cardboard christmas tree ornaments

Why send that cardboard box to the recycling bin when it can be transformed into a beautiful ornament for the tree or holiday window? This is a wonderful project to do with kids on a cold winter day (just help the younger kids with the needle and thread). The customized results are sturdy enough to survive storage for many years and many trees to come.

GATHER

- Pencil
- Christmas-themed cookie cutters
- Scraps of cardboard
- Scissors
- Water-based paints
- Paintbrushes
- Nontoxic glue
- Vintage beads, buttons, glitter, and other found objects
- Yarn, ribbon, or cotton thread
- Needle

CREATE

1. Using the pencil, trace the cookie cutter shapes onto the cardboard pieces.

2. Cut out the shapes and paint designs on them. Allow the paint to dry.

3. Glue the beads, buttons, glitter, and found objects to the ornaments.

4. For each ornament, cut a 6- to 7-inch/ 15- to 17-cm piece of yarn, thin piece of ribbon, or thread.

5. Poke a hole in the top of the ornament with the needle and string the thread through the hole to hang it.

DECKING THE OFFICE HALLS

This holiday season, try to bring the green holiday spirit to the workplace. If your office decorates for the holidays, suggest going beyond the traditional decorations to incorporate some green ideas, such as having coworkers bring in decorations instead of buying new ones or hanging edible or homemade decorations instead of plastic ornaments. And suggest that you and your coworkers give back to the community: start a canned food drive for a local food bank or collect gently used toys or winter clothing and donate them to those in need (see Resources).

feather-nest egg ornaments

These whimsical ornaments will look like magical fairies in the branches of your tree. Children love them.

GATHER

- Sterilized needle (see Note, page 95)
- 12 eggs
- Small bowl
- Paintbrush
- White glue
- Nontoxic silver or gold paint
- Nontoxic glitter (silver or white)
- Scissors
- White feathers
- Cotton thread or fishing line

CREATE

1. Using the needle, carefully make a hole in each end of an egg. Put one end of the egg against your mouth and blow the egg whites and yolk out into a bowl (use them for eggnog, baking, or breakfast). Repeat for each egg.

2. Paint the eggs silver or gold and let dry.

3. Paint a thin layer of glue on each egg and sprinkle on the glitter.

4. Cut the tips off the feathers and glue them to the base of the egg (the tips of the feathers should be pointing upward). Compost the remainder of the feathers or use them as stuffing for Recycled Cashmere Pillows (see page 133).

5. To hang the ornaments, cut a 6- to 7-inch/15- to 17-cm length of thread for each egg, fold it in half, and knot each end. (The knots should be small enough to fit both of them through the top hole.) Using the needle, push both knotted ends through the top hole of the egg. Place two drops of glue over the hole and let dry.

angel doily ornaments

This craft is especially fun for kids, and you may already have most of the materials on hand. For some reason everyone I know has extra doilies hanging around at the bottom of their kitchen drawers. I don't use doilies anymore, but somehow I always find a few in my house every year—they must be from the baked goods that people give me. For the cotton balls in this project, I love using the big pieces of cotton that always come in vitamin and supplement jars. But organic cotton balls are fine, too. Look for angel cutouts or other festive images or family photos to glue to the ornaments.

- Small doilies

- Nontoxic silver or gold paint

- Paint brush

- Organic cotton balls

- Nontoxic glue

- Nontoxic glitter

- Angel image or some other sweet image like a family photo

- Cotton thread

1. Paint the doily silver or gold and allow to dry for 30 minutes.

2. Pick apart the cotton to make it fluffy and glue it to the center of the doily.

3. Put lines or spots of glue on the fluffed cotton and apply the glitter.

4. Let the glue dry and then glue an angel image or photo to the center of the doily.

5. Tie or glue a 3- to 4- inch/8- to 10-cm piece of thread to the top of the doily for hanging.

tea bag ornaments

With a few creative touches, used tea bags can be transformed into surprisingly beautiful earth-friendly ornaments.

GATHER

- Used tea bags
- Nontoxic water-based gold and silver paint
- 2 paintbrushes
- Scissors
- Used origami paper or newspaper (a map or sheet music will also work well)
- Nontoxic glue
- Glitter
- Needle (optional)
- Cotton thread (optional)

CREATE

1. Dry the tea bags overnight, making sure to lay them flat.

2. Paint the tea bags, including the string and tag, gold or silver and let dry.

3. Cut out different shapes and strips of origami paper or newspaper and glue them to both sides of the tea bags. Glue glitter onto each bag. Let dry.

4. Wrap the tea bag string around a Christmas tree branch, or use the needle and thread to sew a loop onto the bag to hang it.

sugared crabapple ornaments

My daughter loves the tiny crabapples that make their appearance during the winter months. When I was a child, my mother would attach a red thread to them and hang them from our Christmas tree, but I decided to add a little sparkle. After Christmas, you can toss them in the compost bin; it's better to wash off the sugar first, but it's not absolutely necessary.

GATHER

- Small, shallow bowl
- Whisk
- 2 egg whites
- 1 tablespoon water
- Crabapples, as many as you would like on your tree (I usually have ten), with their stems
- Scissors
- Red or green thread
- Paintbrush (optional)
- 1 cup/200 g sugar
- Large, shallow bowl

CREATE

1. In the small bowl, whisk together the egg whites and water.

2. For each crabapple, cut one 6-inch/ 15-cm length of thread and tie it to the stem, creating a loop.

3. Dip each crabapple into the egg-white mixture, making sure it is entirely coated. (You can use a paintbrush instead, if you like.)

4. Place the sugar in the large bowl. Roll each crabapple in the sugar, making sure it is completely coated.

5. Hang the crabapples to dry for about 2 hours.

leaf ornaments

What better way to celebrate the planet than by creating leaf ornaments? These delicate decorations add a sparkle to any tree or window. Kids love to get involved in this project, so send them outside to gather various leaves in different shapes. (Autumn is the best time to find them, if you can plan ahead. You also can order leaves from www.paper-source.com.)

GATHER

- Nontoxic gold and silver paint
- Paintbrushes
- Leaves of various shapes and sizes
- Cookie sheet lined with paper (try cutting up used paper bags)
- Nontoxic glue
- Scissors
- Cotton thread

CREATE

1. Paint one side of each leaf and place it on the paper-lined cookie sheet to dry. Turn the leaves over, paint them on the other side, and let dry.

2. To hang, cut 6 to 7 inches/15 to 17 cm of thread for each ornament and tie it in a loop around the end of each stem.

NOTE: *If you have a spool of fishing line to use up, you can use that to hang the ornaments. But don't buy a new roll of fishing line for this purpose; it's made of plastic, so it won't biodegrade, and if it ends up in the trash, it eventually can harm birds and other wildlife by getting tangled in their beaks and feet.*

cranberry and popcorn garland

Popcorn and cranberry garlands are as old as the hills and add so much traditional charm to your tree. Make a big bowl of Parmesan and Yeast Flake Popcorn (page 112) and pop extra corn for the garland. After Christmas, send the kids out with the garland to decorate any shrubs or trees in your garden. They will love watching the birds feast on the garland!

GATHER

CREATE

- **Popcorn, preferably without salt or butter**

- **Scissors**

- **1 spool heavyweight sewing thread (waxed dental floss works well too, because it is less prone to breakage and the wax makes it easier to slide the cranberries on)**

- **1 heavyweight sewing needle**

- **Cranberries (see Note)**

1. After popping the popcorn, let it sit out for a day to get stale; fresh popcorn crumbles.

2. Cut several 3-foot/92-cm lengths of thread (the number depends on how long a garland you want). Tie a knot at one end and thread the other end through the needle. The individual segments can be tied together when you're finished, but be sure to leave a couple of inches/5 cm of thread free at the unknotted end of each segment.

3. Push the needle through one cranberry and slide it down the length of the thread to the knotted end. Repeat with a piece of popcorn. Alternate threading the popcorn and cranberries until the 3-foot/92-cm segment is finished. Have fun with this: you may want to create different patterns, such as 10 pieces of popcorn and then 3 cranberries, etc.

4. Tie the segments together and hang the garland on your tree.

NOTE: *While fresh cranberries are easy to string on the garland, they can be hard to find. I like to use dried cranberries, which add an antique feel to the garland. Don't use frozen cranberries—they will just fall apart.*

twig stars

I always like to turn to nature for inspiring yet simple decorations. These delightful ornaments are made from twigs gathered in the woods or even in your own backyard. Use hemp twine, thread, pieces of fabric, or bits of used ribbon to bind the twig pieces together. Use your imagination to make other shapes as well.

- **White paper (rescued from the recycling bin)**
- **Pencil**
- **Ruler**
- **Dainty twigs about 3- to 4-inches/ 8- to 10-cm long and uniform in diameter**
- **Nontoxic glue gun**
- **Used hemp twine, fabric, or ribbon**
- **Nontoxic tacky glue (optional)**
- **Nontoxic glitter (optional)**

1. Draw the shape of a five-pointed star on the white paper with the pencil and ruler.

2. Place the twigs over the star you've drawn, using it as your guide. Glue the twigs together at the corners with the glue gun.

3. Wait for the glue to dry (2 to 3 minutes), then secure the four lower points of the star with small lengths (2 to 3 inches/ 5 to 8 cm each) of twine, fabric, or ribbon, tying the twine into knots at the points.

4. On the top point, wrap a longer length of ribbon (6 to 7 inches/15 to 17 cm long) and then create a loop from which the star will hang.

5. If you want to add a little bit of sparkle, place a bit of tacky glue on the twigs and sprinkle them with glitter. Let dry.

walnut ornaments

More than any other Christmas decoration, these ornaments remind me of my childhood. I used to sit and watch my mother make them. It looked painstaking, but the result was so worth it. I have left all my mother's walnut ornaments plain, but if you want to add a little color, paint them gold or silver. Use the nut meat for Maple Walnut Cookies (page 113) or Maple Walnuts in Recycled Jam Jars (page 147). That way you are using the entire nut, without any waste.

- **16 whole walnuts in their shells**

- **Nutcracker**

- **Scissors**

- **Green or red cotton thread**

- **Strong nontoxic glue**

- **Nontoxic gold or silver paint (optional)**

- **Paintbrush (optional)**

1. Carefully crack the walnuts in the middle of the nut, along the seam. Open the shells carefully, without breaking them. Remove the nut meat and the inner membranes of the nut.

2. Cut one 5- to 6-inch/13- to 15-cm length of thread for each ornament.

3. Carefully run glue along the edge of a nut half. Fold one piece of thread into a U and lay the ends of the thread at the top of the nut half. Gently place the other half back on, and press the two halves closed.

4. Repeat with the remaining walnuts. Allow to dry overnight.

5. When the glue has dried, you can paint the walnuts if you like. Hang the ornaments to dry for 3 to 4 hours.

apple, cranberry, and brie quesadillas with black bean salsa

This is the perfect appetizer, a true crowd pleaser. The tart apples and sweet cranberries combine perfectly with the spice of the black bean salsa. Plus, this dish is super-easy to make. The black bean salsa can be made a day in advance and refrigerated.

| SERVES 6 TO 8 |

- 1 can (15 ounces/420 g) black beans
- 1 tablespoon minced fresh cilantro
- 1 scallion (white part only), finely sliced
- 1 tablespoon minced red onion
- ½ green or Thai chile, minced
- 2 Roma tomatoes, diced into ¼-inch/6.5-mm cubes
- Salt and pepper to taste
- 8 ounces/225 g chilled Brie, thinly sliced
- 4 flour tortillas
- 1 medium Fuji apple, peeled and thinly sliced
- ¼ cup/65 g dried cranberries

1. In a small bowl combine the black beans, cilantro, scallion, red onion, chile, tomatoes, salt, and pepper. Mix well and set aside.

2. Place three slices of Brie on one half of one tortilla, spaced about ½ inch/1.25 cm apart. Lay slices of apple across the brie slices on the tortilla (you'll need about 6 slices). Top with 5 or 6 dried cranberries. Fold the filled tortillas in half to create a semi circle. Repeat with remaining tortillas and ingredients.

3. Heat a grill pan on medium heat and place the tortillas in the pan. Weigh them down with a small metal lid. Cook for 3 to 4 minutes on each side, until the cheese is melted and the apples are somewhat soft.

4. Cut each tortilla into 4 to 6 wedges and serve with the black bean salsa.

cranberry turkey tramezzino

A *tramezzino* is an Italian sandwich, and what better way to use leftover cranberry sauce and turkey meat?

| SERVES 6 TO 8 |

- 1½ teaspoons olive oil
- 1 small yellow onion, thinly sliced
- 6 ounces/170 g (12 tablespoons) mayonnaise
- 4 to 6 slices whole wheat bread
- 6 ounces/170 g (12 tablespoons) cranberry sauce
- Freshly cracked black pepper to taste
- 10 to 15 fresh sage leaves
- 4 to 6 slices turkey
- 3 to 4 slices Monterey Jack cheese

1. Heat a small nonstick pan over medium heat. Add the olive oil and then the onions. Sauté until the onions are translucent, about 5 minutes. Lower the heat to medium-low and continue cooking for 25 to 30 minutes, stirring occasionally, until the onions are caramelized.

2. For each sandwich, spread a thin layer of mayonnaise on one slice of bread. Spread a thin layer of cranberry sauce on the other slice and sprinkle with pepper. Place 5 sage leaves over the cranberry sauce, followed by 2 slices of turkey and 1½ slices of cheese. Top with a thin layer of caramelized onions and place the slice with mayonnaise on top. Repeat with remaining ingredients.

3. Heat a grill pan on medium-high heat. Grill each sandwich 2 to 3 minutes on each side, until the cheese is melted, placing a metal lid on the sandwich to press it down.

4. Remove the crusts and cut each sandwich into 4 rectangular pieces. Serve hot.

parmesan and yeast flake popcorn

Popcorn is the perfect snack to munch on while trimming the Christmas tree. As a matter of fact, it's a great tree decoration as well. This popcorn is addictive; I have been known to eat an entire bowl in one sitting. Nutritional yeast flakes, sold in health food stores, make the popcorn even healthier: they are a great source of protein and are rich in B-vitamins.

| MAKES ABOUT 13 CUPS |

- 2 tablespoons canola oil
- ½ cup/75 g popcorn kernels
- 2 tablespoons unsalted butter, melted
- ½ cup/15 g finely grated Parmesan cheese
- 2 tablespoons nutritional yeast flakes
- 2 teaspoons salt

1. Put the canola oil and popcorn kernels in a large pot. Cover and turn the heat to medium.

2. When the first few popcorn kernels pop, begin to shake the pot vigorously, making sure to hold onto the lid.

3. Continue until the sounds of the popping slow down and the pot is full of popped kernels. Turn off the heat and add the melted butter, Parmesan, yeast flakes, and salt. Toss until well mixed.

maple walnut cookies

These cookies are so good you can't eat just one, so make a double recipe. They taste even better dunked in a mug of hot cocoa. You can use fresh walnuts in the shell if you like; just crack the shells gently, and save them to make Walnut Ornaments (page 108). If you can't find walnuts, you can substitute pecans. Whatever kind of nut you use, be sure to look for organic ones; pesticides such as diazinon and endosulfan are used frequently in nut production, especially in the United States and India. (See Resources for an organic nut source.) Dare I say these make great Christmas gifts?

| MAKES ABOUT 2 DOZEN COOKIES |

- 2¾ cups/340 g all-purpose flour
- 2 teaspoons baking powder
- ½ teaspoon salt
- 2 sticks (1 cup/225 g) unsalted butter, at room temperature
- 1 cup/220 g packed brown sugar
- ½ cup/100 g sugar
- 1 large egg
- 2 teaspoons maple extract
- ½ cup/65 g walnuts, finely chopped

1. In a medium bowl, combine the flour, baking powder, and salt and set aside.

2. In a large bowl, beat the butter and both sugars with an electric mixer on medium speed (or with a whisk) until fluffy and light, about 3 minutes.

3. Add the egg and maple extract and mix on medium speed until well combined, scraping down the sides of the bowl. Add the dry ingredients and nuts and mix on low or with a spoon until well combined.

4. Divide the dough in half and form two logs about 2 inches/5 cm in diameter. Wrap the dough logs in parchment paper and chill in the refrigerator until the dough is firm, at least 1 hour.

5. Preheat the oven to 350°F/180°C (Gas Mark 4). Line a baking sheet with parchment paper.

6. Slice the dough logs into ½-inch-thick / 1.25-cm-thick circles and place them 2 inches/5 cm apart on the baking sheet.

7. Bake for 15 to 16 minutes, or until the edges are brown. Let cool before serving.

chai hot cocoa with whipped cream

A mug of steaming hot chocolate is a much-beloved holiday treat, and I like to dress up ordinary cocoa with my own recipe for chai, an Indian spice blend. Hot cocoa isn't as sinful as you might think: scientists have found that dark chocolate is loaded with antioxidants called flavonoids. They help the body destroy free radicals, which are harmful molecules that cause many ailments, such as heart disease. Look for organic fair-trade cocoa powder, such as Green & Black's brand, available in many grocery stores.

| SERVES 4 |

FOR THE CHAI HOT COCOA

- 3 cups/750 ml milk
- 1 cup/250 ml water
- 3 tablespoons cocoa powder
- 2 tablespoons sugar (optional; see Note)
- 2 cinnamon sticks
- 5 cardamom pods
- ½ teaspoon ground ginger
- Pinch cayenne pepper
- Pinch ground cloves
- 2 teaspoons pure vanilla extract (or 1 vanilla bean)
- 4 ounces/110 g bittersweet (60 percent cacao) chocolate (see Note)

FOR THE WHIPPED WREAM

- 2 cups/500 ml heavy cream
- 2 tablespoons sugar
- 1½ teaspoons pure vanilla extract
- Pinch salt

TO MAKE THE CHAI HOT COCOA:

1. Combine the milk, water, cocoa powder, sugar (if using), cinnamon sticks, cardamom pods, ginger, cayenne, cloves, and vanilla in a large saucepan. Heat over medium heat until scalding. Remove from heat and let steep for 10 minutes, then strain into a bowl or pitcher.

2. Transfer the milk back to the saucepan and heat over medium-high heat to scalding. Add the chocolate and stir for 5 minutes, just until chocolate is melted.

3. Strain again and pour into 4 mugs. Top with a dollop of whipped cream.

NOTE: *If you're using chocolate that contains 70 percent cacao, add 2 tablespoons sugar. (The higher the percentage of cacao solids, the more intense and less sweet the chocolate is.) Almost all good-quality chocolate producers list the percentage of cacao on the label.*

TO MAKE THE WHIPPED CREAM:

1. Place a mixing bowl and the beaters of an electric mixer in the refrigerator or freezer for at least 15 minutes.

2. Pour the cream, sugar, vanilla, and salt into the chilled bowl and whip on high speed until soft peaks form.

giving

Giving gifts is one of the joys of the season: seeing a face light up with surprise and appreciation is so satisfying. It is particularly **gratifying** if you've created the gift yourself. And as the gift giver, it is a wonderful way to introduce friends and family to a lifestyle that you're enthusiastic about. Demonstrating what giving really means, whether it's creating a gift using your hands or making a **donation** to a charity in someone else's name, makes the act that much more meaningful.

Creative gift ideas can be inspired by virtually anything. I saw a beautiful bag in a fashion magazine and re-created it using a vintage bag and recycled buttons and brooches. Advertisers want you to get the newest and latest of everything, but think about the **sentimental** value of your gift, which can be much more important. Plus, every time we buy something new, we're creating more waste; that's just the way it is.

I'm often asked for advice about what to do with unwanted environmentally unfriendly holiday gifts. I'm a big believer in **re-gifting**. I ask myself, Should I give away this soap that contains phosphates, or throw it away? I give it away, because I know someone else will enjoy it, and that's much better than having the soap end up in a landfill. Ultimately it's up to the individual and his or her own philosophy, but regardless, I always feel blessed that I received something to begin with.

But to avoid receiving unwanted gifts in the first place, you have to let your friends and relatives know that you're going green. You'll see—people will eventually stop giving you gifts that aren't green.

ONLINE *or* ON FOOT:
WHICH IS BEST FOR THE PLANET?

There is much debate about whether online shopping is environmentally friendly. Since holiday shopping usually involves several trips to different stores, it requires a lot of gas (and if you're shipping the gifts, the toll on the planet is even higher). The greenest option is to buy all your gifts at once, from one place. It's even better if you can walk or take public transportation to the store. But if that's impossible, buy online from a source that is eco-conscious about its products and packaging, such as www.greenfeet.com (see Resources).

You don't have to entirely eliminate online shopping. Here are some ways to shop smarter—and greener—on the web:

- Do your best to order from responsible companies (see Resources).

- Never use the overnight shipping option, because air freight is a much bigger source of pollution than ground transportation.

- Have items delivered to your office, since the delivery companies will stop there anyway; that will eliminate a single trip made to your home, as well as any redelivery attempts if you're not there. Residential deliveries require more driving than deliveries to commercial establishments, according to UPS.

- Alternatively, consolidate your order and ship it all to one location: rather than sending ten gifts to ten addresses, you can send the gifts to the home of the person hosting the Christmas celebration. I do this every year with my family; I send gifts to my in-laws' home, because I know the extended family will open presents at their house on Christmas morning.

- If you plan to order a few gifts from the same web site, order everything at once, which will reduce packaging and minimize transportation costs.

- Don't print out shipping or order confirmation forms; download them to your computer instead.

TREELESS GREETINGS

The 2.65 billion Christmas cards sold each year in the United States could fill a football field ten stories high, according to use-less-stuff.com, and they require the harvesting of nearly three hundred thousand trees. (And those with foil or gold coating can't be recycled.) As this Web site also points out, if each American sent one card fewer, we'd save fifty thousand cubic yards of paper. Here's another startling statistic: for every pound of virgin paper made from tree pulp, about one pound of carbon dioxide is emitted.

This year, consider sending holiday e-mails or e-cards instead. (For a few fabulous e-card Web sites, see Resources.) If you must send cards, choose ones that are printed on recycled paper. Look for cards with the recycled paper symbol, a high percentage of postconsumer content (the fiber in paper can be recycled up to a dozen times before it becomes too short for papermaking, according to Conservatree.com), and the PCF (processed chlorine free) logo, which indicates that no further chlorine bleaching of the recycled source paper has occurred.

Or send a card that keeps on living: a biodegradable card from Bloomin' Flower Cards. You can plant the whole card in a pot or in the ground, and the embedded seeds will grow. Made with soy-based inks, renewable hemp, and 100 percent postconsumer content, these cards are green in every sense of the word, and the joy they spread will last long after the holidays are over.

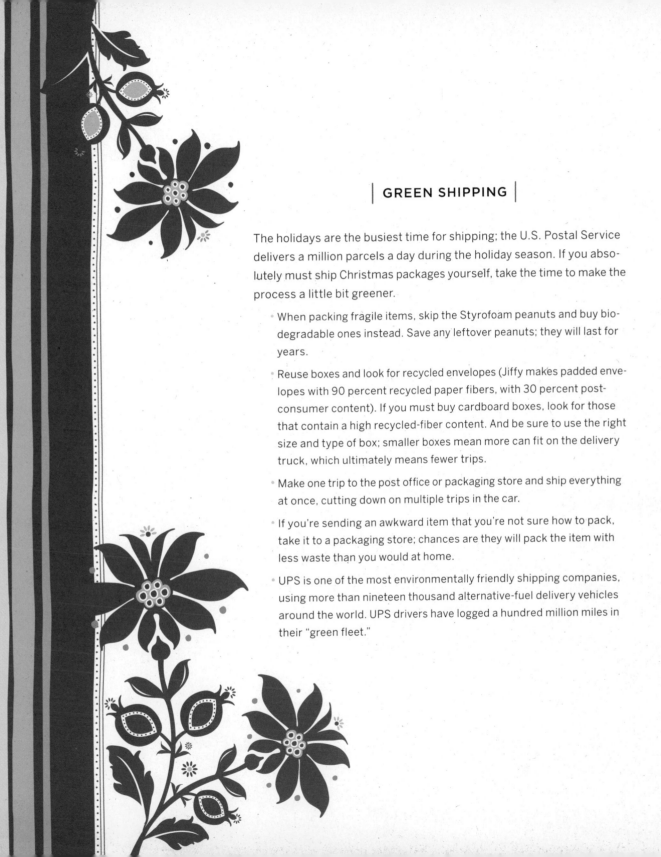

GREEN SHIPPING

The holidays are the busiest time for shipping; the U.S. Postal Service delivers a million parcels a day during the holiday season. If you absolutely must ship Christmas packages yourself, take the time to make the process a little bit greener.

- When packing fragile items, skip the Styrofoam peanuts and buy biodegradable ones instead. Save any leftover peanuts; they will last for years.

- Reuse boxes and look for recycled envelopes (Jiffy makes padded envelopes with 90 percent recycled paper fibers, with 30 percent postconsumer content). If you must buy cardboard boxes, look for those that contain a high recycled-fiber content. And be sure to use the right size and type of box; smaller boxes mean more can fit on the delivery truck, which ultimately means fewer trips.

- Make one trip to the post office or packaging store and ship everything at once, cutting down on multiple trips in the car.

- If you're sending an awkward item that you're not sure how to pack, take it to a packaging store; chances are they will pack the item with less waste than you would at home.

- UPS is one of the most environmentally friendly shipping companies, using more than nineteen thousand alternative-fuel delivery vehicles around the world. UPS drivers have logged a hundred million miles in their "green fleet."

tea box gift tags

The paper stock used for tea boxes is the perfect thickness for quality gift tags. Some of the boxes are so pretty, too; Yogi Tea boxes (shown in photo at left) are printed on the inside with beautiful Indian designs.

GATHER

CREATE

- Pencil
- Christmas-themed cookie cutters
- Empty tea boxes
- Scissors
- Hole punch
- Used hemp twine or ribbon
- Nontoxic gold paint
- Paintbrush
- Nontoxic glue
- Small rhinestones

1. With the pencil, trace the cookie-cutter shapes on the empty tea boxes and cut out the shapes.

2. Use the hole punch to make a hole at the top of the tag, lace the twine or ribbon through it, and knot.

3. Paint the reverse side of the tag with gold paint. Let the tag dry and glue on the rhinestones.

EXPERT GREEN TIP

SUMMER RAYNE OAKES, *model-activist and author of* Style, Naturally: The Savvy Shopping Guide to Sustainable Fashion & Beauty

www.summerrayneoakes.com

The holiday season for me is more about a time for giving than it is for receiving. My mother and I used to head over to the local church, hospital, or school to pick up "grab bag" gift requests for families in need. We'd have an incredible time picking out clothes for the kids, but the most precious gifts were the ones my mother would hand-knit. I remember handmade scarves, caps, and gloves making their way into the boxes on many occasions. If you are like me and don't have the time or skill to make something, give the gift of handmade by buying wares on a Web site, such as Etsy.com, where artisans sell their goods.

recycled christmas card gift tags

In the United States alone, 2.2 billion Christmas cards are sent every year, according to Hallmark Cards, Inc. And most Christmas cards are printed on virgin paper. Give the cards you receive extra life: use them to make these fun gift tags. They are a great gift themselves, too: make thirty tags, place them in a small tin, and give it to a friend as an early holiday present.

 GATHER

 CREATE

- **Pencil or pen**
- **Christmas-themed cookie cutters**
- **Used Christmas cards**
- **Scissors**
- **Hole punch**
- **Used hemp twine or ribbon**

1. With the pencil or pen, trace the cookie-cutter shapes on the Christmas cards and cut out the shapes.

2. Use the hole punch to make a hole in the tag. Lace the twine or ribbon through the hole, and knot.

EXPERT GREEN TIP

LYN LEAR, *founder, the Environmental Media Association*

www.ema-online.org

In gifts as well as life, it's what's inside that counts, of course, but there is something about a beautifully wrapped present that shows you care enough to give it extra personal attention. I love using dried flowers and leaves to make each gift one of a kind, instead of using the same old ribbons and bows. And, of course, recycling gift paper is an absolute must among the "eco-chic"! To save even more paper, it's wonderful to give something that hardly needs to be wrapped up more than slipping it into an envelope: theater or concert tickets, a notice of a donation to your friend's favorite charity, or even a "voucher" to spend a special day together, redeemable at any time.

block-printed shoe bag gift wrap

Plain fabric shoe bags get a makeover with a paint block design and make a sturdy, reusable bag for almost any gift. Don't feel limited by shoe bags; you can do this on any fabric, or even paper. Look for printing blocks at art supply stores, craft stores, or on eBay. If you don't receive shoe bags with your shoe purchases, you can find organic cotton or hemp produce bags online at www.reusablebags.com.

GATHER

CREATE

- **Nontoxic fabric paint**
- **Large old plate**
- **Paint roller**
- **Vintage India printing blocks (or other vintage printing blocks), found at flea markets or online**
- **Fabric shoe bags**

Pour the paint onto the plate. Roll the paint roller through the paint and then roll it over the print block. Stamp the design onto each shoe bag, stamping twice if desired. Let the shoe bags dry completely.

NOTE: *You can also apply this technique to recycled brown paper and use it as wrapping paper.*

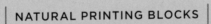

| NATURAL PRINTING BLOCKS |

The greenest printing blocks of all are those you make at home. Cabbages, potatoes, leaves, and sponges make beautiful natural patterns that can be used for homemade Christmas cards, wrapping paper, gift bags, or gift tags. Here are a few ways you can make your own blocks:

- Potatoes: Cut the potatoes in half and, using a knife, carefully carve a design on the flat surface. Dip the potato stamp in nontoxic paint to decorate. When you're finished, wash off the paint and throw the potatoes in the composter.
- Cabbage: Cut a head of cabbage crosswise into wedges, so you can see the inner designs of the cabbage leaves. Dip the flat surfaces in nontoxic paint to decorate. When you're finished, wash off the paint and throw the cabbage in the composter.
- Leaves: Find beautiful veiny leaves and lightly coat one side with nontoxic paint; press the painted leaves onto paper or fabric. When you're finished, wash the paint off and throw the leaves in the composter.
- Sponges: Cut flat surfaces onto a sea sponge or other natural sponge and dip them in nontoxic paint to create beautiful designs.

newspaper gift wrap and bows

I stopped my newspaper subscription years ago and get all my news online. But some people still love sitting with a cup of coffee and reading the morning paper. Here is a great way to reuse your newspaper. The store advertisements are the most festive and colorful. Just use the paper as you would ordinary gift wrap. You also can make lovely bows with the newspaper. Here's how:

 **GATHER**

 **CREATE**

- **Old newspapers**
- **Tape**

1. Cut out 10 strips about 7 inches/17 cm long and 1 inch/2.5 cm wide.

2. Fan out the strips evenly over the gift in an asterisk shape. Place a piece of tape in the middle of the asterisk, taping the strips together and to the gift.

3. Create a loop with each strip and tape them down to the gift. You can always add more strips, loop them, and tape them to the gift too.

| ALL WRAPPED UP |

If every family in the United States wrapped three gifts in something other than store-bought wrapping paper, it would save enough paper to cover forty-five thousand football fields, according to the Sierra Club. Wrapping paper is almost never recyclable, because of the low quality of the paper fibers and the large amounts of ink used to decorate the paper. If you're a paper nut, look for wrapping paper made from hemp, kenaf (a plant native to Africa), tree bark, or grasses that are harvested without pesticides, don't require the use of chlorine bleach, and create minimal environmental impact. If nothing else, conserve resources by buying half-used rolls of wrapping paper at a thrift store. Old or used gift wrap can be shredded and used as cushioning for shipping packages.

Don't forget the tape: "green" tape is PVC (polyvinyl chloride) free. Most cellophane or Scotch tape is made with the petroleum-based PVC, which releases carcinogens during the manufacturing process. Natural rubber tape and gummed paper tape are the green alternatives to standard tape (check art supply stores). An even better option is to skip the tape altogether and secure the wrapping paper with twine, ribbon, or yarn.

If you can't give up traditional wrapping, at least replace the gift box with a reused gift bag. Because gift boxes almost always use tissue paper as well, a gift bag (sans tissue) is better. And the gift bags are easier to store, so you can reuse them. Recycled-paper gift bags and cloth bags are both excellent options.

Get really creative with your wrapping: try using a bag that the recipient can reuse often, such as a cotton or canvas bag. Baskets and glass jars also make fun yet useful gift "boxes." Match the wrap to the gift theme: wrap kitchen tools in a set of kitchen towels. Old sheet music, maps, magazine pages, calendar pages, and posters also make eye-catching wrapping paper.

EXPERT GREEN TIP

PETER GLATZER, *creator/executive producer,* "Alter Ecó"

For the past few years, I've been wrapping my gifts in old newspaper and tying it closed with twine. This wasn't an eco decision; I'm just a bachelor who never has wrapping paper around. There's something old-fashioned and utilitarian about the aesthetics of a bottle or a box wrapped in old newspaper, and the twine makes it feel more like a gift. I tend to favor the *New York Times* financial pages. The stock index works the best. There are no ads, no headlines, and there's a uniform pattern to it. Maybe there's some ironic connection between the reuse factor of financial-page wrapping paper and the new numbers on the Dow Jones, but then again, maybe I'm reading into it too much. Anyway, it looks swell, it's getting an extra usage out of the newspaper, and there's an extra layer of thought to whatever the gift is inside.

MORE GREEN GIFT WRAP IDEAS

After years of buying conventional wrapping paper and bows, it may seem daunting to completely overhaul the way you wrap gifts. But getting creative with wrapping makes your gifts more personal and meaningful—and it's more fun. Here are some of my favorite ideas:

- Use recycled kraft paper, plain brown paper made from 100 percent recycled and 20 percent postconsumer waste. Personalize the gift wrap by drawing on it or rubber-stamping it. Kraft paper is available in most paper stores and online at www.papernuts.com.

- Remember that not every item needs to be wrapped! Large items need only a reused ribbon or bow and a Recycled Christmas Card Gift Tag (page 124).

- Pack gifts in antique tins found at garage sales.

- Use Christmas stockings as gift wrap.

- If you're giving away a bottle of wine, just tie a piece of reused ribbon around it—no need for the decorative plastic bag.

- Get inspired by household items: in Japan, one of the greenest countries in the world, it's traditional to use a square of cloth called *furoshiki* to wrap presents. Use any scrap cloth you have in the house: old scarves, bandanas, shirts, or pillowcases. Place the gift in the middle of the fabric and gather the ends at the top. Secure with ribbon or use fabric glue to create a patchwork of fabric.

- Tear pages from magazines to make great wrapping paper. Tailor the magazine-wrap to your recipient's interests. For example, if your sister likes fashion, use pages from a fashion magazine. Don't go out and buy magazines for this, though; use old ones you have lying around, or ask a salon or doctor's office to set the old ones aside for you instead of throwing them out.

- T-shirt gift wrapping has two functions, and it's easy to make. Turn an old T-shirt inside out and sew the bottom of the shirt closed. Turn the shirt right-side out and push gifts in through the neck hole. Tie the top of the shirt closed with the sleeves. After your recipient opens the gift, he or she can reuse the shirt wrapping as a carry-all sack.

- Create a tradition of reusing gift wrap year after year. Make it a rule: no virgin paper gift wrap, ever.

- Decline the gift wrapping offered by stores—you can do it at home greener.

- If you do use a store's gift boxes or gift wrap, request that that the store provide boxes and wrapping made from postconsumer recycled paper. Big businesses will supply them if we demand them.

decorative gift box

Revive gift boxes from Christmases past with postcards, cardboard pieces, ribbons, lace, colorful paint, glitter, and other odds and ends.

GATHER

- Pencil
- Ruler
- Corrugated cardboard
- Scissors or X-acto knife
- Nontoxic water-based acrylic gold paint
- Paintbrush
- White glue
- Postcard or photograph
- Used gift box (the size depends on the size and type of gift going into it)
- Gold ribbon
- Red ribbon

CREATE

1. With the pencil and ruler, measure and draw six strips on the corrugated cardboard. The size of the strips will depend on the size box you are using. Cut them out with the scissors or X-acto knife, paint them gold, and let dry.

2. Glue the postcard or photograph onto the top center of the gift box's lid.

3. Glue the strips of gold-painted cardboard to the outer edges of the box.

4. Cut two lengths each of gold and red ribbon (long enough to wrap around your box) and wrap the ribbons around the box.

| REUSE YOUR RIBBON |

A big red bow is the classic Christmas-gift symbol, but most of those bows, which are made of plastic and acrylic, end up in the trash and then sit in landfills for hundreds of years. According to use-less-stuff. com, if every family reused just two feet of holiday ribbon, thirty-eight thousand miles of ribbon would be saved—enough ribbon to wrap around the planet.

If you can't bear to give a gift without a bow, remember that ribbon isn't the only way to finish a gift; raffia and hemp twine are beautiful green alternatives (see Resources). Save every beautiful ribbon you receive and reuse it; most ribbon can be used a few times before it gets frayed and worn. For ribbon storage tips, see page 167.

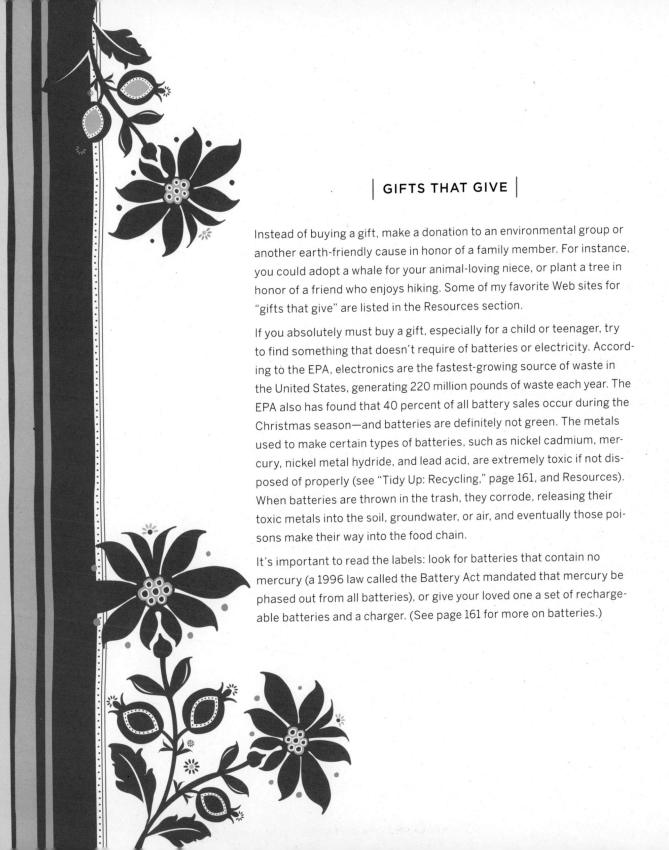

GIFTS THAT GIVE

Instead of buying a gift, make a donation to an environmental group or another earth-friendly cause in honor of a family member. For instance, you could adopt a whale for your animal-loving niece, or plant a tree in honor of a friend who enjoys hiking. Some of my favorite Web sites for "gifts that give" are listed in the Resources section.

If you absolutely must buy a gift, especially for a child or teenager, try to find something that doesn't require of batteries or electricity. According to the EPA, electronics are the fastest-growing source of waste in the United States, generating 220 million pounds of waste each year. The EPA also has found that 40 percent of all battery sales occur during the Christmas season—and batteries are definitely not green. The metals used to make certain types of batteries, such as nickel cadmium, mercury, nickel metal hydride, and lead acid, are extremely toxic if not disposed of properly (see "Tidy Up: Recycling," page 161, and Resources). When batteries are thrown in the trash, they corrode, releasing their toxic metals into the soil, groundwater, or air, and eventually those poisons make their way into the food chain.

It's important to read the labels: look for batteries that contain no mercury (a 1996 law called the Battery Act mandated that mercury be phased out from all batteries), or give your loved one a set of rechargeable batteries and a charger. (See page 161 for more on batteries.)

recycled cashmere pillows

I love reassigning jobs to things that were meaningful in my life. These pillows are easy to make with a sewing machine. If you don't have a machine, try to borrow one or do a trade with a friend: she helps you sew some pillows, and you bake her a batch of cookies. You can use any kind of wool sweater, but cashmere is the softest. These pillows look cute on a bed or on couches in a family room.

- 3 cashmere sweaters (any color you want, but I used red, heather gray, and dark gray)
- Scissors
- Tacky glue (Crafter's Pick makes a great one; see Resources)
- Sewing machine
- Black thread
- 2 vintage buttons
- Needle
- Dark gray thread
- Clear thread
- Organic cotton balls
- Old pillow stuffing
- Sequins, lace, buttons, or other decorative items (optional)

1. Cut a 10-by-14-inch/25-by-35-cm rectangle out of the red and heather gray sweaters, and then a 3½-by-3½-inch/ 9-by-9-cm patch from each of the same sweaters.

2. Cut two 2-by-2-inch/5-by-5-cm square patches from the dark gray sweater.

3. For the front side of the pillow, place one drop of tacky glue at the center of the heather gray rectangle. Center the red square over the glue and press it down.

4. Place a drop of tacky glue in the center of the red square. Center the dark gray square over the red square and press it down on the glue. Let dry.

5. For the back side of the pillow, place one drop of tacky glue at the center of the red rectangle. Center the heather gray square over the glue and press it down.

6. Place a drop of glue in the center of heather gray square. Center the dark gray square over the heather gray square and press it down on the glue. Let dry.

7. Once the two sides are dry, use zigzag stitching and black thread to sew each square patch onto the rectangular piece of cashmere.

8. Place a button on the center of each dark gray square and hand-sew it on with dark gray thread.

9. Place both sides of the pillow against each other, inside out, with the buttons facing each other.

10. Use zigzag stitching and the clear thread to sew approximately ¼ inch/ 6.5 mm in from the outer edges on all four sides, leaving approximately 2 inches/ 5 cm on one side open, for stuffing.

11. Turn the pillow right-side out.

12. Stuff the pillow with organic cotton balls and pillow stuffing.

13. Turn the top edges of the 2-inch/ 5-cm gap inward and pull them together; use the clear thread to hand-stitch the gap with small, tight stitches. Get creative: sew sequins, lace, buttons, or other decorative items to the pillow.

recycled t-shirt pot holders

I wish I could say I dreamed up this idea myself, but I did not. I saw potholders similar to these in an eco-lifestyle store, and I just loved them. This is my version. T-shirts with cool designs make the best pot holders. You can sew these by hand, but a sewing machine is definitely your best bet.

GATHER

- **3 T-shirts in different colors**
- **An old sweater**
- **Scissors**
- **Different colored thread**
- **Sewing machine**

CREATE

1. Cut two layers of T-shirt in 4½-by-4½-inch/11-by-11-cm squares. Use a different color T-shirt for each square.

2. Cut one layer of sweater in a 4½-inch/11 cm square.

3. Cut a strip of T-shirt 3 to 4 inches/8 to 10 cm long by ¾ inch/1.9 cm wide, to make a hanging loop.

4. Center the sweater square over one square of T-shirt. Sew a running stitch about ¼ inch/6.5 mm in from the edge of the sweater around the perimeter of the square, to sew it and the T-shirt square together.

5. Sew circular and zigzag patterns back and forth across the layers of fabric. Be playful with the stitching.

6. Center the second T-shirt square over the first on the other side of the sweater. Sew another running stitch about ¼ inch/6.5 mm in from the edge around the perimeter of square. Using a different color thread from the first, sew circular and zigzag patterns back and forth across the T-shirt layers.

7. Sew the strip of T-shirt in a loop onto the corner of the pot holder.

vintage button clutch

Revive a simple black clutch with vintage buttons and brooches. This lovely clutch is both sophisticated and fun.

- **One clutch purse**
- **12 to 15 buttons or broaches**
- **Needle**
- **Thread**

Sew the buttons on the clutch, and pin on the brooches.

NOTE: *Another great way to use old brooches is with vintage scarves: Tie one around your waist, pin the brooch to the knot, and make a sassy sash.*

HOMEMADE GREEN GIFT BASKETS

How often do you end up with gift baskets full of things you don't eat or use? Here are some ideas for personalized gift baskets that are sure to please. And for packaging, don't just stick to baskets. Use old crates, boxes, tins, or any fun flea-market find to hold the gifts. Skip the cellophane wrap and cover your gift basket with recycled fabric, or just finish it with a bow.

- The Chocoholic's Delight: Create a tin of organic and fair-trade chocolates. Include hot cocoa and baking chocolate too, and add a chocolate recipe book for fun.
- Clean and Green: Encourage a loved one to get rid of toxic cleaning products. Fill a tin pail with eco-friendly kitchen and bathroom cleaners, laundry detergent, and natural sea sponges.
- "Intro to the Green Life": Introduce a family member to a whole new world. Fill a recycled canvas bag with a gift certificate to a carbon-offset program, a DVD of the documentary *An Inconvenient Truth*, and my friend Josh Dorfman's book, *The Lazy Environmentalist*. Provide them with a list of cool green sites, like Ecofabulous.com, treehugger.com, and sprig.com, and include some of your favorite green products, such as eco-friendly cleaners, organic chocolates, or an organic cotton T-shirt.
- Teatime: Fill a basket with organic loose-leaf (it reduces paper use) fair-trade teas. Include a mesh tea ball and two vintage teacups.

cuff links

Guys can be so hard to get gifts for, but my husband always appreciates a fun pair of cuff links. You'll need cuff-link backs (see Resources); strong, nontoxic glue; and vintage buttons, seashells, old computer or typewriter keys, or other small found objects. Choose a decorative pair of objects, glue each one to a cuff-link back, and let dry.

| GREEN GIFT INSPIRATION |

Get creative and give gifts that keep on giving.

- Pass on a book you enjoyed with a note about how much you liked it.
- Make a homemade "gift certificate" for a neighborly chore or friendly favor.
- Give someone a membership to a gym or a museum, or a pair of tickets to a sporting event, the theater, or the symphony.
- Visit flea markets and vintage stores for unusual items that will surprise your friend and grant the item yet another life.
- Give a music lover a gift certificate to iTunes or any online music store.
- Make a family photo album or DVD.
- Consider a gift card for a finicky friend or family member, to avoid giving an unwanted gifts. Look for gift cards printed on "bioplastics": Target uses a biodegradable plastic made from corn sugar for its gift cards; called Mirel, the bioplastic eventually breaks down, instead of enduring in a landfill for up to four hundred years, like standard gift cards.
- Throw a white elephant party, which is green by definition, because you're giving away things you don't want. Call it a green elephant party instead, and tell guests they must bring something reused, recycled, or remade.
- Keep boxes (both gift and shipping) and break them down to be reused.

| CHILDREN'S GIFTS |

Some of these gifts you can put together from what you have already. Others you can look for used. Either way, these gifts foster the "green" in children.

- Make paper-bag puppets: Use recycled lunch bags, googly eyes, markers or crayons, ribbon scraps, and buttons to create funny puppet faces.

- Put together a necklace-making kit for a young girl: Buy old beaded necklaces and bracelets at a flea market, cut the beads off the strands, and gather them in an old tin with a roll of hemp twine.

- Buy a gift membership to a nature institute and help foster a child's relationship to the outdoors.

- Give gently used secondhand books.

- Make an eco-conscious paint kit with nontoxic paint, wood-handled brushes with natural bristles, and postconsumer recycled paper.

- Stuff a basket with dress-up clothes: Buy a large basket and fill it with your fun old clothes, or head to the local Goodwill for colorful hats, scarves, gloves, ties, and dresses. My daughter plays dress-up for hours with hers.

- Cultivate the green thumb in a child you know with the gift of a gardening kit. Seeds, gloves, and gardening tools collected in a basket make a perfect gift.

- Go on Craigslist or eBay and look for used musical instruments. You can get a great deal.

bottle cap refrigerator magnets

These cute magnets make perfect stocking stuffers or advent-calendar markers. You can make an entire set of magnets using family photos, or choose themes like animals, botanical prints, or movies. This also is a great opportunity to put your stamp collection to good use.

GATHER

- Scissors
- Used wrapping paper
- Bottle caps from glass bottles (without dents)
- White glue
- Small photographs, stamps, or little drawings
- Nontoxic glitter
- Magnet strips (you'll need one magnet strip for each bottle cap, available at craft and office supply stores)

CREATE

1. Cut small circles out of the wrapping paper to fit inside each bottle cap. Glue them to the insides of the bottle caps.

2. Cut a photograph, stamp, or other picture into a small rectangle and glue it to the paper inside a bottle cap.

3. Run a thin line of glue around the photograph. While the glue is still wet, sprinkle the glitter over the glue and shake off the excess. Repeat for each bottle cap magnet.

4. Glue a magnet strip to the back of each bottle cap and let them dry overnight.

pumpkin butter and tamari-roasted pumpkin seeds

I like to give my friends a gift basket with these two festive holiday treats: creamy pumpkin butter and crunchy pumpkin seeds. They make a healthful, festive treat and a nice change from holiday cookies. Tamari, a type of soy sauce, adds rich flavor to the crunchy seeds.

pumpkin butter

| MAKES 5 TO 6 CUPS |

- 2 cans (15 ounces/420 g each) pumpkin puree
- ¾ cup/180 ml apple cider or apple juice
- ½ teaspoon ground nutmeg
- ¼ teaspoon ground cloves
- 2 teaspoons ground cinnamon
- 2 teaspoons ground ginger
- 1¼ cups/250 g caster (superfine) sugar
- ¼ cup/60 ml pure maple syrup

tamari-roasted pumpkin seeds

| MAKES 1 CUP |

- 8 ounces/225 g (1 cup) pumpkin seeds
- 2 tablespoons tamari

TO MAKE THE PUMPKIN BUTTER:

1. Place all the ingredients in a heavy-bottomed pot, stir to combine, and bring to a boil over medium-high heat, uncovered.

2. Reduce heat to low and simmer 40 minutes, stirring frequently.

3. Ladle the hot pumpkin mixture into sterilized jars, leaving ¼ inch/6.5 mm of space at the top of the jar. Remove any air bubbles by gently shaking the jars, and wipe the rims of the jars. Cover tightly with the lids.

4. Submerge the jars in a large pot of water; the water level should reach to 1 inch/2.5 cm above the tops of the jars. Bring the water to a boil and boil the jars for 10 minutes, to seal them. Remove the jars from the pot using tongs and let cool.

5. The jars can be stored in a cool, dark cupboard for up to 6 months. Once opened, the pumpkin butter will last in the refrigerator for up to 2 weeks.

TO MAKE THE PUMPKIN SEEDS:

1. Heat a large pan on high heat.

2. Add the pumpkin seeds and stir briskly to prevent burning until some of the seeds begin to lightly brown, about 5 minutes. Add the tamari and mix until the seeds are coated.

3. Remove the pan from the heat and keep stirring for 1 more minute. Transfer the seeds to a bowl and let cool.

4. The seeds can be stored in an airtight container in a cool, dark cupboard for up to 6 months.

seven layers of sin bars

The name of this recipe says it all: chocolate, pecans, dried fruit, and coconut come together for a decadent treat. These make great a gift for anyone with a sweet tooth. When I was younger and living on a struggling actor's budget, I would make these for friends, agents, and associates and drive around the city, dropping off little boxes of sinful goodness. Everybody loved them.

| MAKES ABOUT 24 BARS |

- 3½ cups/320 g graham cracker crumbs (one 14½-ounce box of graham crackers, mashed into crumbs)
- 2 sticks (1 cup/225 g) unsalted butter, melted
- 1½ cups/105 g finely shredded unsweetened coconut
- 1 cup/150 g chocolate chips
- 12 ounces/330 g pecans, roughly chopped
- ½ cup/135 g dried cranberries, roughly chopped
- ½ cup/135 g dried apricots, roughly chopped
- 1 can/14 ounces/390 g sweetened condensed milk

1. Preheat the oven to 350°F/180°C (Gas Mark 4). Spray a 9-by-13-inch/23-by-33-cm jelly roll pan with nonstick spray. Cover the pan with a piece of parchment paper and spray the paper with nonstick spray.

2. In a medium bowl, mix together the graham cracker crumbs and butter until well combined.

3. Transfer the graham cracker mixture to the jelly roll pan and create a crust about ⅓ inch/8.5 mm thick on the bottom of the pan, pressing the mixture down firmly with the back of a spatula. Make sure the crust is firm and uniform.

4. To make the layers, sprinkle a handful of shredded coconut evenly over the crust, followed by a handful of chocolate chips, then the pecans, dried cranberries, and dried apricots. Drizzle about ¼ cup/60 ml of the condensed milk evenly over the top. Continue layering with the remaining ingredients, finishing with the condensed milk.

5. Bake, uncovered, for 15 to 20 minutes, until the chocolate chips have melted and the edges are golden. Let cool in the jelly roll pan for 1 hour.

6. Chill the bars in the refrigerator for 2 hours, uncovered. (This will make the bars easier to cut.)

7. Cut the bars and serve immediately, or transfer them to gift tins or boxes.

maple walnuts in recycled jam jars

These sweet nuts look beautiful packed into recycled jam jars. Spoon a few walnuts over waffles or pancakes or pour them over vanilla ice cream or plain yogurt.

| MAKES 4 JARS |

- 2 cups/250 g shelled walnuts
- 4 glass jars, 8 ounces/250 ml each
- 2 cups/500 ml pure maple syrup

1. Divide the walnuts evenly among the glass jars. Pour ½ cup/125 ml syrup into each jar and close the lids tightly.

2. Partially submerge the jars in a large pot of water; the water should come half-way up the jars. Bring the water to a boil and boil the jars for 10 minutes, to seal them. Remove from the water and let cool.

3. The walnuts can be stored in a cool, dark cupboard for up to 4 months. Once the jar is opened, the walnuts will keep in the refrigerator for up to 6 weeks.

BAMBOO-STEAMER CARRYING TRAYS

DANNY SEO, Green Lifestyle Guru, from *Simply Green Giving*, (Harper Collins, 2006. Reprinted with permission.)

www.dannyseo.com

The problem when traveling with freshly baked treats is that decorative trays do a poor job at protecting the goodies from breakage, and food storage containers do a poor job at being decorative. The solution is a Chinese bamboo steamer. Not only is it attractive and effective at protecting food, it can also be a gift.

Most bamboo steamers can be found at good kitchen supply stores or at an Asian market. They come in a variety of sizes and tiers; larger ones can accommodate pies and tarts and smaller ones can be used to carry cookies, hors d'oeuvres, and other smaller treats. Fill each tier with different treats and stack the steamer trays on top of each other. Wrap a decorative ribbon around the whole thing to keep it together.

celery root soup with crumbled bacon and humboldt fog cheese

This winter soup is the ideal starter to Christmas dinner. The smoky flavor of the celery root goes hand in hand with the salty crumbled bacon and the tangy Humboldt Fog, a lovely cheese made in Northern California with milk from some of the best goat herds in the country. Be sure to use nitrate-free organic bacon.

| SERVES 6 TO 8 |

- 2 tablespoons unsalted butter
- 1 large yellow onion roughly chopped
- 4 medium celery roots (about 2 pounds/900 g total), peeled and cut into 1-inch/2.5-cm cubes
- ½ cup/90 g peeled and cubed russet potatoes (make 1-inch/2.5-cm cubes)
- 5 cups/1.25 L chicken broth
- ¼ cup/60 ml heavy cream
- Salt and pepper to taste
- 6 strips bacon (preferably nitrate-free)
- 2 ounces/60 g Humboldt Fog cheese (or other soft goat cheese), finely crumbled

1. Melt the butter in a large pot over medium heat. Add the onions, celery root, and potatoes and sauté 5 minutes, stirring often.

2. Add the broth, bring to a boil, reduce heat to low, and simmer, uncovered, 25 to 30 minutes, stirring occasionally, until celery root is tender when poked with a fork.

3. Transfer the soup to a blender and puree in batches if necessary, then return the pureed soup to the pot. Or, use an immersion blender and puree the soup in the pot. Add the cream, salt, and pepper.

4. Fry the bacon until it's extra crisp, about 10 minutes, turning occasionally. Set aside and let cool. Break the bacon into finely crumbled pieces.

5. Serve the soup in individual bowls and top each serving with bacon bits and crumbled cheese.

GLOBAL GREEN:

| CHRISTMAS IN FRANCE *(Joyeaux Noël)* |

The French, famous for their love of fine cuisine, celebrate Christmas with many special dishes in a tradition that combines family, community, and respect for the planet. After attending midnight mass, many French families celebrate *un Réveillon*: an all-night feast at home or in a restaurant that has stayed open for the occasion. The menu always draws from specific regional ingredients: the epitome of eating seasonally and locally.

brussels sprouts with currants, shallots, and bread crumbs

The first time I made this dish for certain young members of my husband's family, who swore they hated brussels sprouts, they walked away from the table mighty surprised, and I was pleased to clear away their empty plates. This hearty side dish is simply brussels sprouts spruced up in a fancy dress; the sweetness of the apples and the currants balance out the tartness of the sprouts. The toasted bread crumbs add a crunchy "wow."

| SERVES 8 TO 10 |

- 4 tablespoons unsalted butter

- 1 cup/50 g bread crumbs

- 2 pounds/900 g brussels sprouts

- 4 small shallots, chopped

- 2 small Fuji apples, peeled and chopped into ¼-inch/6.5-mm cubes

- 2 teaspoons minced fresh thyme

- 1 cup/270 g currants

- Juice of 1 large lemon (about 4 tablespoons)

- Salt to taste

- ½ cup/7 g fresh flat-leaf parsley, finely chopped

1. Melt 2 tablespoons butter in a small saucepan over low heat. Add the bread crumbs and sauté, stirring constantly, until brown, about 4 minutes. Set aside in a small serving bowl.

2. Cut the brussels sprouts into ⅛-inch/3-mm slices, starting at the top of the head and working down toward the root. (The slices will resemble ribbons.)

3. Melt the remaining 2 tablespoons butter in a large sauté pan over medium high heat and add the shallots. Sauté 2 to 3, minutes until shallots are translucent. Add the brussels sprouts and cook for 10 minutes, until softened. Add the apples and thyme and cook for 5 more minutes. Add the currants, lemon juice, and salt, and stir to combine. Stir in the parsley.

4. Serve the brussels sprouts warm, with bread crumbs passed separately. (You don't want the bread crumbs to be soggy, so invite your guests to sprinkle the crumbs on their brussels sprouts at the table.)

pan-fried chicken breasts with chestnut stuffing and port gravy

This dish is fancy enough for a holiday gathering, but easy enough to prepare when you've got a houseful of guests. Rich chestnuts are one of my favorite winter ingredients.

| SERVES 6 TO 8 |

CHICKEN WITH CHESTNUT STUFFING

- 6 tablespoons unsalted butter
- 1 cup/160 g finely diced celery ribs
- 1 cup/180 g finely diced onion
- 6 to 7 fresh sage leaves, minced
- 1 jar (7 ounces/200 g) chestnuts, chopped into ¼-inch/6.5-mm pieces
- 1 slice hearty bread, diced into ¼-inch cubes
- ½ cup/125 ml chicken broth
- 6 boneless, skinless chicken breasts
- Salt and pepper to taste
- 4 tablespoons olive oil, for cooking

PORT GRAVY

- 2 tablespoons unsalted butter
- 1 cup/180 g finely diced onion
- 2 tablespoons all-purpose flour
- 3 sprigs fresh thyme
- 1¾ cups/425 ml chicken broth
- 1 cup/250 ml port wine
- 1 tablespoon heavy cream
- Salt to taste

TO MAKE THE CHESTNUT STUFFING AND CHICKEN:

1. Melt 2 tablespoons butter in a heavy-bottomed saucepan over medium-high heat. Add the celery and onion and cook for 10 minutes, until softened. Add the sage and cook for another 2 minutes. Add the chestnuts and bread and cook for 20 minutes, stirring occasionally.

2. Lower the heat and add the chicken broth. Stir the mixture until the broth is absorbed, 4 to 5 minutes. Remove from heat.

3. Preheat the oven to 375°F/190°C (Gas Mark 5).

4. Wash the chicken breasts and pat dry. Slice them horizontally, creating a crevice. Be careful not to cut all the way through. Stuff each breast with stuffing, distributing it evenly among all 6 breasts. Season each breast with salt and pepper.

5. Heat two heavy-bottomed pans on medium heat. Drizzle 2 tablespoons olive oil in each and add 2 tablespoons butter. When the butter has melted and the pans are hot, gently place 2 or 3 chicken breasts in each pan. Cook them for 3 minutes, or until the bottom is browned. Turn the chicken breasts over and cook for another 2 to 3 minutes.

6. When all the chicken is browned, place the chicken breasts on a large baking sheet and bake for 8 to 10 minutes, until the juices run clear.

TO MAKE THE PORT GRAVY:

1. Melt the butter in a saucepan on medium heat and add the onion. Sauté until the onion is translucent, about 5 minutes.

2. Whisk in the flour until no lumps remain. Add the thyme, chicken broth, and port wine and bring to a boil. Boil for 5 minutes to reduce the liquid, then reduce the heat to medium-low and simmer, uncovered, for 10 minutes.

3. Remove from heat and strain through a fine-mesh sieve. Transfer the sauce back to the pan and whisk in the cream. Season with salt.

pumpkin gnocchi
with browned sage butter

Gnocchi, little Italian dumplings traditionally made with potatoes, become light and airy when made with pumpkin and ricotta. Sage adds another winter flavor to this cozy dish.

| SERVES 6 TO 8 |

- 1 can (15 ounces/420 g) pumpkin purée
- 8 ounces/225 g fresh ricotta cheese
- 7 tablespoons extra-fine bread crumbs
- 14 tablespoons all-purpose flour
- ½ teaspoon ground nutmeg
- Salt and pepper to taste
- 2 large eggs, beaten
- 1 tablespoon butter
- 4 fresh sage leaves, minced
- Grated Parmesan cheese, for garnish

1. Lightly flour a baking sheet and set aside.

2. In a small saucepan over high heat, boil the pumpkin puree for about 2 minutes. Transfer to the bowl of a food processor and puree until smooth. Let cool.

3. In a large mixing bowl, combine the ricotta, bread crumbs, flour, nutmeg, salt, and pepper.

4. Add the eggs to the pumpkin puree and pulse until just combined. Add the pumpkin mixture to the ricotta-flour mixture and stir until just combined. Knead the dough briefly in the bowl

5. Roll the dough into 1-inch-/2.5-cm-wide logs. (The dough will be a bit sticky, so use a good amount of flour on your hands when rolling out the dough logs.) Wrap the logs in plastic wrap and put them in the freezer for 10 minutes.

6. Cut the frozen logs into ½-inch-/1.25-cm-thick rounds. Transfer the gnocchi pieces onto the floured baking sheet and freeze for at least 20 minutes.

7. Bring a medium pot of water to a boil and cook the gnocchi until it floats to the top, about 3 minutes. Remove the gnocchi from the pot with a slotted spoon.

8. Melt the butter in a sauté pan on medium heat until it browns. Add the sage and the gnocchi and sauté until gnocchi are lightly golden, about 2 minutes. Serve immediately, garnished with the Parmesan.

mashed sweet potatoes with ginger and mascarpone

Sweet potatoes are at their peak in the wintertime, so they make an ideal holiday vegetable. Despite its sweetness, this casserole is a perfect side dish for Christmas dinner. Although I must admit, it's tasty enough to eat as a dessert!

| SERVES 6 TO 8 |

- 2 pounds/900 g garnet yams, peeled and cubed into 2-inch-5-cm cubes
- 4 tablespoons unsalted butter
- 2 teaspoons peeled and grated fresh ginger
- ½ cup/110 g packed brown sugar
- 1 teaspoon ground cinnamon
- ½ teaspoon ground nutmeg
- 1½ teaspoons salt
- 1 cup/8 oz. mascarpone
- 2½ cups/125 g mini marshmallows (see Note)
- ½ cup/65 g pecans, toasted and roughly chopped (see Note)

1. Preheat the oven to 375°F/190°C (Gas Mark 5).

2. Place the potatoes in a large pot on a steamer tray with about 2 inches/5 cm of water. Steam until the potatoes are tender when poked with a fork, 15 to 20 minutes.

3. Transfer the potatoes to a large bowl and mash to a rough mash.

4. In a small pan over low heat, melt the butter and add the ginger. Sauté for 2 to 3 minutes and add the brown sugar, cinnamon, and nutmeg. Stir until sugar is melted, about 4 minutes. Pour the butter mixture into the potato mash, add the salt, and stir until combined.

5. Add the mascarpone to the potato mixture and stir until well combined. Transfer the mixture to a 9-by-13-inch/23-by-33-cm baking dish. Sprinkle the marshmallows over the top and cover them with the pecan pieces.

6. Bake, uncovered, for 10 to 15 minutes, or until the marshmallows are golden.

NOTE: *Most marshmallows are full of preservatives and artificial ingredients, but all-natural marshmallows made from sugar, gelatin, and vanilla extract are available in some grocery stores and bakeries.*

Toasting pecans is a great way to bring out their flavor. All you need is a heavy-bottomed pan and high heat. When the pan is nice and hot, add the pecans and stir them vigorously until they begin to brown, 4 to 5 minutes. Remove them from the heat and set them aside till you're ready for them.

mini apple strudels with brown sugar whipped cream

Strudel is a classic German pastry but is very time-consuming to make. This is a simplified version that still has all of the delicious flavor of a traditional strudel.

| SERVES 6 TO 8 |

FOR THE CRUMBLE

- ½ cup/65 g chopped organic walnuts
- ¼ cup/55 g brown sugar
- 1 tablespoon graham cracker crumbs
- Pinch salt

FOR THE FILLING

- 4 medium Fuji apples, cored and cut into ¼-inch/6.5-mm cubes, about 3 cups/550 g cubed
- Juice of 1 small lemon (about 2 tablespoons)
- ⅓ cup/90 g currants
- 3 tablespoons sugar
- 1½ teaspoons vanilla extract
- ¼ teaspoon salt
- ½ teaspoon ground cinnamon
- 1½ tablespoons unsalted butter

FOR THE STRUDEL

- 4 to 5 sheets phyllo dough, cut into 3½-inch/9-cm squares (will be 6 to 8 squares per sheet)
- ½ cup/110 g unsalted butter, melted

FOR THE BROWN SUGAR WHIPPED CREAM

- 1½ cups/375 ml whipping cream
- 1 tablespoon brown sugar
- 1 teaspoon vanilla extract

1. Preheat the oven to 350°F/180°C (Gas Mark 4). Spray 6 to 8 muffin cups with nonstick cooking spray and set aside.

TO MAKE THE CRUMBLE TOPPING:

2. Combine the walnuts, brown sugar, graham cracker crumbs, and salt in the bowl of a food processor and pulse until a fine crumb forms. Set aside.

TO MAKE THE FILLING:

3. In a medium bowl combine the apples, lemon juice, currants, sugar, vanilla, salt, and cinnamon and mix thoroughly. Melt the 1½ tablespoons butter in a large saucepan over medium heat and add the apple mixture. Cook the apples until soft, about 20 minutes. Remove from the heat and set aside.

4. Lightly brush each sheet of phyllo with the melted butter. Divide the sheets evenly into the prepared muffin cups. Each strudel should have 4 to 5 layers of phyllo.

5. Divide half the crumble between the muffin cups and then top with the apple mixture. Top with the remaining crumble and bake for 25 to 30 minutes, until phyllo and crumble are brown.

TO MAKE THE BROWN SUGAR WHIPPED CREAM:

6. Place a mixing bowl and the beaters of an electric mixer in the refrigerator or freezer for at least 15 minutes. Pour the cream and sugar and vanilla extract into the chilled bowl and whip on high speed until soft peaks form. Serve the strudel warm with a dollop of whipped cream.

cranberry prosecco cocktail

There simply isn't a more festive beverage than this pink cocktail. Tart cranberries and Italy's answer to champagne, prosecco, combine to make a tasty, not-too-sweet party drink.

| SERVES 6 |

- 1 cup/270 g frozen cranberries, thawed
- ¼ cup/50 g sugar
- 1 bottle (750 milliliters) prosecco, chilled (champagne or sparkling wine can be substituted)

Place the cranberries and sugar in a bowl and macerate for at least 1 hour, or up to 6 hours. Stir the berries occasionally, lightly mashing them. Place 1 tablespoon of macerated berries in each of six champagne flutes. Fill the flutes with prosecco and serve.

| GREEN PARTY TIP |

One of my favorite decorating ideas comes from New Mexico, where luminarias line the paths of homes and businesses during the Christmas season. Luminarias, essentially candles in paper bags, are not only green, they're simple to create. Take one package of recycled-paper lunch bags and fill each bag with two to four inches/10 cm of sand. Embed a soy or beeswax tea light candle securely in the sand. Line the bags along your walkway, staircase, or front porch one to two feet apart, and light the candles (check on them every so often to make sure they haven't caught fire; the risk of fire is very low). If you like, you also can punch star designs in one side of the bag; hand punches are available at craft stores.

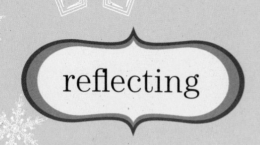

reflecting

After the parties are over, Santa has come and gone, and the dust has settled, it's time to take a moment to reflect on the holiday. Rather than rushing into the excitement of the New Year, take the time to reuse, recycle, and reframe all the Christmas "waste."

The British celebrate a distinctive holiday the day after Christmas: December 26 is Boxing Day, a tradition that began in the nineteenth century, when the members of a household staff, who worked on Christmas Day, were given gifts by their employers. They traveled home on their day off with their "Christmas boxes."

Why not incorporate that spirit into your own holiday? Instead of rushing to the mall to return or exchange gifts, designate December 26 as a "reflecting" day: Collect unwanted gifts and donate them to a local charity; plan a relaxing meal with friends or family and serve leftovers from the previous day's feast; take a few minutes to collect any gift wrap (iron it on low heat, if you're planning to reuse it) and ribbon and organize it for next year; make a file folder for Christmas cards, or gather them in an envelope and donate them (see Resources). Plant the Christmas tree (if you bought a living tree) or Christmas plant in a large pot, so it can grow until the ground is soft enough to plant it outdoors. There are so many ways to reflect on the bounty of the holiday and ensure that the benefits are enjoyed well into the New Year.

I've found that to successfully recycle or reuse items, it's crucial to have a system. Establish a "go-to" green Christmas section in your home, labeling everything clearly. By establishing a space and keeping everything in easy-to-access bins, you're much more likely to get organized and stay organized.

tidy up: recycling

Take a day or two after the holidays to sort through the Christmas bounty and recycle or give away what you don't need. Here's a list of leftover items that are particularly common after the holidays.

BATTERIES: There are two types of batteries, single-use and rechargeable. Americans throw away 180,000 tons of batteries each year, according to www.earth911.org. The most common single-use batteries are alkaline batteries, the kind that power toys, flashlights, etc. Each state has its own regulations about how to dispose of used batteries. California passed a law in 2006 that classifies all batteries, including alkaline batteries, as hazardous waste and mandates that they be disposed of in one of three ways: at a recycling center, at a hazardous waste center, or through a universal waste handler. Even if you live in an area where you can dispose of batteries in your household trash, you should never throw away groups of batteries at once, because if they are not completely dead, they could come in contact with one another and create safety problems.

Rechargeable batteries, such as those for laptops, cell phones, and power tools, can be recycled (see Resources). Check your local recycling programs (electronics stores like Best Buy often have recycling programs), and see Resources.

BROKEN HOLIDAY LIGHTS: If you're feeling creative, remove the bulbs from all the lights (disposing of them properly) and use the strands for art projects. Unfortunately, though, these usually end up in the garbage.

CHRISTMAS CARDS: St. Jude's Ranch for Children has a Recycled Card Program, in which children create new greeting cards out of old ones, and the profits go to the ranch, which works to prevent child abuse. Collect cards from friends, family, and neighbors as well. St. Jude's accepts cards from any occasion. For more information, go to www.stjudesranch.org/give/Recycled_Cards.php.

COFFEE GROUNDS: The holidays often require a healthy dose of caffeine, but don't toss those coffee grounds into the trash can. Coffee grounds are a great nitrogen boost to plants and compost piles (after brewing, the grounds contain 2 percent nitrogen). If you're not a coffee drinker but would like to give your garden a boost, you can pick up grounds at many coffee shops; Starbucks has a "Grounds for Your Garden" program that offers free bags of used grounds. Coffee grounds also make a great nontoxic fertilizer: mix a half-pound of coffee grounds with five gallons of water.

OLD CLOTHES: Other than repurposing a clothing item (such as turning old cashmere sweaters into Recycled Cashmere Pillows), the best thing to do is donate unwanted clothes. Many charities accept clean clothing; some focus on particular types of clothes, such as coats or business attire (see Resources). Many charities take clean bedding as well.

PACKING PEANUTS: Some packaging stores will be happy to take clean packing peanuts off your hands. Call the Plastic Loosefill Council's Peanut Hotline at 1-800-828-2214; they will direct you to a local store that will reuse the peanuts. Or, bag them and keep them to use for your own future shipping.

RIBBON: To keep ribbons looking pretty and ready for the next package, wrap them around empty cores from toilet paper or paper towels.

SHOES: The best way to recycle shoes is either to donate them to those in need—there are several charities that distribute new and gently used shoes—or send them to the shoe manufacturer; many shoe companies collect used shoes and recycle them. Nike is a leader in this effort, taking all brands of sneakers and turning them into athletic surfaces like basketball courts (see Resources).

STYROFOAM: Some communities recycle Styrofoam that comes with TVs, appliances, and other electronics. Look for local recycling options before loading it into the trash bin.

CHRISTMAS TREES: Instead of putting your Christmas tree in the trash, recycle it or, better yet, compost or mulch it (the greenest option). Some cities offer tree recycling programs, but you also can go to www.earth911.org to find a tree recycling program near you. For more on Christmas trees, see page 86.

WRAPPING PAPER: Recyclable wrapping paper can be recycled as long as it doesn't have tape on it (tape contains nonrecyclable elements). Nonrecyclable wrapping paper, which is anything with foil, decoration, or dyes on it, cannot be recycled and must be put in the trash. To preserve a pretty piece of wrapping paper for another occasion, iron the paper on low heat and store it between two sheets of cardboard. (For more on reusing wrapping paper, as well as plenty of ideas for alternatives to the usual wrapping paper, see chapter 4.)

| CONTAINERS |

Save any decorative cookie or candy tins you receive and use them for your own holiday baked goods next year. Or, use them to store household items like rubber bands, coins, etc.

I keep all takeout containers to give away leftovers at parties or to pack cookies. Dress up the containers with used ribbon and encourage your recipient to reuse the container, too. When I receive jam as a gift, I always keep the jar and use it for storage, or I reuse it when I make Maple Walnuts in Recycled Jam Jars (page 147) or Pumpkin Butter (page 144).

---

composting christmas

Composting is the planet's natural recycling program. You add materials from around the house that you used to consider garbage, and they will decompose into feasts for worms and microbes and give you rich soil for your garden. By composting, you're using your waste to create more life. You must learn how to compost correctly, or you'll just be creating a toxic dump in your backyard, but composting is not as daunting as it sounds: you're basically throwing stuff in a bin and mixing it with other stuff, rather than tossing it in the garbage can. Composting does take time, though; it will take between six and twelve months for your composter to produce the dark brown, nearly black material that you can add to the soil in the garden.

The holiday season is a great source of composting material. Starting a compost pile in the winter isn't ideal, because compost must be kept dry and because you'll have more grass clippings and other greenery in the spring. But if you already compost, the holidays produce plenty of material that can be returned to the life cycle by being composted.

You can visit www.compostguide.com for helpful information and tips on composting, but here are some basics to get you started. The first thing you need is a composter, which you can buy or make yourself. There are many on the market: tumblers, grates, bins, pods, even glorified garbage cans. Research the various types online or at a local garden shop and decide which one suits your needs and space requirements; just be sure it has a lid. You also can make a composter with stakes and chicken wire or recycled wooden pallets. Binding, screwing, or wiring four wooden pallets together to make a box creates an easy, functional composter and keeps the pallets out of the landfill. (A local grocery, furniture, or lumber store, or even a large electronics outlet, may be happy to get rid of its old wood pallets.) My composter is a simple wooden box with slats to allow air to circulate.

The next step is choosing a location for your composter. Use a well-drained, level spot, away from walls or wooden fences. If possible, keep the composter away from trees, too, because their roots will seek the moisture and nutrients in your compost pile. You'll need to set aside four or five square feet or one and a half square meters of space; the more space you have, the easier it is to access it.

Once you have your composter set up, it's imperative that you learn how to use it correctly. First, lay down a base layer of branches and twigs about six inches/15 cm deep. (You can even use a wooden pallet for the base layer.) This will help air circulate under the material you will add to the composter: proportionate layers of brown and green material.

Pay careful attention to your holiday waste; much of it is compostable, such as any wreath made from evergreens or other greens, cut flowers, and plants.

The green layer can include:
- Grass cuttings
- Tea leaves (including the bag, if it's made of organic recycled material)
- Coffee grounds
- Dead flowers
- Weeds (leaves only; no roots or seeds)
- Old plants
- Seaweed, green material from ponds, algae

The brown layer can include:
- Wood material, prunings, wood chippings (shredded, if possible)
- Coffee grounds
- Recycled brown paper, cardboard, paper-towel rolls (shredded, if possible)
- Leaves (small quantities)
- Eggshells and paper egg cartons (rinse and crush first)
- Sawdust, wood shavings, pinecones
- Hay and straw (small quantities)
- Clothes dryer lint, pet and human hairs
- Uncooked kitchen scraps that are plant-, vegetable-, or fruit-based, without any oils

The following should never be added to your composter:
- Meat or fish
- Grease, oil, cooked food scraps
- Cat litter
- Manure
- Diapers
- Barbecue ash

There's no shortage of kitchen scraps around the holidays, and these scraps are either green or brown material, depending on what you're cooking. Set aside a bin in your kitchen for collecting food-prep scraps. It doesn't have to be large; I use a stainless steel bucket with a lid, which I keep on the kitchen counter within easy reach. Use the list provided, paying particular attention to what not to include, and start collecting your scraps. (No cooked food can be added to a compost pile, because it lacks the necessary enzymes that break it down.) When the container is full, simply empty the bin into your composter and mix it in. If you're just getting started and the composter is empty, you'll need to toss in some grass clippings to cover your kitchen scraps to deter pests.

| MAKING THE MOST OF LEFTOVERS |

Holiday parties, dinners, and celebrations produce a bounty of delicious food, and although most of it ends up in our bellies, much of ends up in the garbage: 28 billion pounds of edible food ends up in landfills between Thanksgiving and New Year's Day. Here are a few easy ways to keep more food out of the trash (and more cash in your wallet) this holiday season:

- Try to get an accurate head count if you'll be entertaining (encourage guests to RSVP, or follow up by phone yourself), so you won't shop and cook for thirty people and have only fifteen show up.

- Send guests home with leftovers that they can enjoy the next day.

- Get creative in the kitchen: go online and find recipes that use your leftovers.

- Before dropping off food gifts, make sure the recipient can or will enjoy them (many people suffer from food allergies or are on restricted diets). Think about how many boxes of cookies, candies, and other holiday treats end up in the trash—you wouldn't want to add to those!

- Donate excess canned food to a local food bank.

GETTING ORGANIZED, *staying* ORGANIZED

- Label all storage boxes with a detailed list of their contents.

- Create a specific box or container with broken down gift boxes, wrapping paper, tissue paper, gift bags, and ribbons for next year. Having an organized location will make you more likely to keep these in good condition so you can enjoy using them next year. Invest in storage containers to store Christmas items. Metal ones are best, but tin cubbies or wicker baskets will work; use plastic bins as a last resort. I used to think I was becoming a pack rat by saving everything, but it's all about coming up with a system and labeling things.

- Keep like decorations together: keep fragile ornaments in one box, nature-inspired ornaments in another, etc.

- Consider storing fragile decorations in plastic containers or metal bins, instead of in cardboard boxes.

- Pack heavy decorations separately from lightweight ones. If you'll be stacking the boxes, be sure to put the lightweight, fragile decorations on top.

- Label storage boxes with instructions, to make unpacking easier. For example, if you hang certain decorations or ornaments first, write that on the box: "Open this box first."

- Separate Christmas supplies by their materials. Put strings, ribbons, and homemade displays in separate boxes.

- Remove all compostable material from wreaths (fruits, vegetables, and garlands) before storing.

- Cover your Christmas wreaths and other hanging decorations carefully with a recycled plastic bag, and hang them somewhere or lie them flat in a box, so they won't get crushed.

- Wrap candles individually in tissue paper left over from Christmas gifts and keep them in one box.

- Separate indoor and outdoor decorations. Put them in different colored boxes, or label them with different colored markers.

- Store Christmas linens in a suitcase, to reduce the risk of mold or moth damage. Include a naturally scented or homemade sachet to keep the linens smelling fresh.

Resources

General Green Living

These are some of my favorite resources for green living and inspiration.

ECOFABULOUS

www.ecofabulous.com

Founded by the "Queen of Green," Zem Joaquin, this site features reviews of the best eco-products on the market. The site offers a wealth of other information as well, including "Eco-Lingo," which defines the often-confusing green terms.

ENVIRONMENTAL MEDIA ASSOCIATION

www.ema-online.org

This group works with celebrities and businesses to educate the public about environmental issues. They provide a "Green Seal" program to help you reduce your carbon footprint, tips for green living, and many helpful green links.

GLOBAL GREEN

Globalgreen.org

This nonprofit was created by Diane Meyer Simon as the United States branch of Mikhail Gorbachev's international organization Green Cross International, and its primary objective is to halt the progress of climate change by building green buildings and cities. The Web site offers a wealth of information on green building, climate solutions, and sustainability.

GLOBAL STEWARDS

www.globalstewards.org

This site offers tips and real-life solutions for greening your life. It covers a wide range of topics, including finding green hotels, reducing junk mail, conserving water, and packing a waste-free lunch.

HEALTHY CHILD, HEALTHY WORLD

www.healthychild.org

This nonprofit works with parents, teachers, and educators to help create more healthful environments for children through education and advocacy. Its comprehensive Web site has an extensive resources section with links to articles, videos, a glossary, and state and federal environmental policies.

H3 ENVIRONMENTAL

http://h3environmental.com

Founded by environmental consultant Mary Cordaro, this company sells organic bedding and mattresses and other healthful home products.

IDEALBITE: A SASSIER SHADE OF GREEN

www.idealbite.com

This Web site and blog has a hip vibe and provides daily eco-tips on everything from food and wine to local environmentally conscious events.

THE LAZY ENVIRONMENTALIST

www.lazyenvironmentalist.com

Started by entrepreneur Josh Dorfman, this Web site (and his book of the same name) offers valuable tips on green living with "no guilt-trips and never any sacrifice," as Josh says. A blog, radio show, and dozens of links will keep you surfing this site for all the green ideas you can imagine.

LIME: HEALTHY LIVING WITH A TWIST

www.lime.com

Run by the retailer Gaiam, Inc. (see page 171), this site offers green tips on everything from yoga to the home to the planet. The site also links to LIME web television, podcasts, and a blog.

SUBURBAN PEOPLE ARE INTO GREEN

www.sprig.com

This site for the style-conscious green citizen focuses on green tips, features, and products for fashion, home, and beauty.

TREEHUGGER

www.treehugger.com

One of the best environmental sites out there, TreeHugger features product information and green solutions on everything from food and health, to travel and nature, to design and architecture, to celebrity and culture. Its podcasts and web videos are very informative.

USE LESS STUFF

http://use-less-stuff.com

This is a great general resource for information on how to reduce waste.

Gifts

ALTERNATIVE GIFT REGISTRY

www.alternativegiftregistry.org

This Web site, run by the New American Dream, a nonprofit that works for both conservation and social justice, offers a gift registry for all occasions featuring alternative gifts such as fair-trade household items like throws and recycled glass tumblers, environmentally friendly electronics, and gift certificates to green hotels. The site also offers advice on planning a sustainable celebration with a comprehensive resources section.

AMERICAN FOREST

www.americanforest.org

A wonderful organization, American Forest allows you to plant trees in the name of a recipient.

CHANGING THE PRESENT

www.changingthepresent.org

This Web site offers charitable gift options arranged by cause, such as disaster relief, education, or HIV/AIDS. You can "buy" a project, such as De-mine a Playing Field or Adopt a Dolphin. Run by ImportantGifts, Inc., the site acts as a grant provider to the charities.

ECO-ARTWARE

http://ecoartware.com

This is a great source for environmentally friendly gifts for men, women, children, and pets.

FORESTSAVER.COM

www.forestsaver.com

This company creates notebooks, note cards, and more out of New York City subway maps.

GLOBAL GIVING

www.globalgiving.com

This is another alternative gift-giving site that connects donors to projects. Choose from a wide variety of projects, including helping disaster victims in Myanmar, retrofitting "dirty" vehicles in the Philippines, providing education to AIDS orphans in Uganda, and helping rural Ethiopians get access to clean water.

GREENFEET: THE PLANET'S HOMESTORE

www.greenfeet.com

This is a great resource for a wide variety of environmentally friendly gift ideas, from bags and books to water filters and hemp dog collars.

GREENGIFTGUIDE.COM

www.greengiftguide.com

Run by the California Department of Conservation, this Web site offers tips on green decorating for every occasion and links to other sites offering green gifts.

LOYALE CLOTHING

www.loyaleclothing.com

This eco-fashion company started by Jenny Hwa offers designs for men, women, and children that use only organic cotton and wool. The company is eco-conscious from the packaging to the materials and even created "seasonless" styles to avoid the traditional gap (e.g., buying fall clothes in August) in fashion seasons.

ORGANIC BOUQUET

www.organicbouquet.com

Through this web site you can have beautiful organic flower arrangements delivered anywhere in the United States.

Eco-Friendly Toys

HUGG-A-PLANET

www.huggaplanet.com

This is the place for pillow globes of the earth and other fun, huggable toys.

MAGIC CABIN

www.magiccabin.com

Here you can buy all-natural, battery-free toys for children of all ages.

PEACE TOYS

PeaceToys.com

This Web site sells a variety of organic toys.

ROSIE HIPPO'S TOYS AND GAMES

www.rosiehippo.com

Rosie Hippo offers hundreds of toys made from wood and other natural materials.

Christmas Trees

To find an organic tree farm in your area, visit one of the following Web sites.

ECO BUSINESS LINKS GREEN DIRECTORY

www.EcoBusinessLinks.com

On this Web site you'll find listings for green businesses, including retailers for gifts and clothing, garden and building supplies, office supplies, and food.

FRIENDS OF THE URBAN FOREST

www.FUF.net

This San Francisco organization is dedicated to planting and protecting trees in San Francisco neighborhoods and offers seasonal information about where to buy Christmas trees.

LOCALHARVEST

www.localharvest.org

This is a directory of local and organic food sources.

ORIGINAL LIVING CHRISTMAS TREE COMPANY

www.LivingChristmasTrees.org

This tree company based in Portland, Oregon, "rents" trees to residents in the Portland area: they drop off and pick up living Christmas trees.

YULE TREE FARMS

http://christmastreeoregon.com/buylivetree.php

This Oregon farm sells live trees. It has been operating since 1964 and is active in conservation efforts.

Tree Recycling

To find a tree recycling program near you, go to www.earth911.org.

Cutting Your Own Christmas Tree

To help thin forests and prevent wildfires, the Bureau of Land Management and the U.S. Forest Service offer permits for cutting your own Christmas tree. For information, visit www.BLM.gov or www.FS.fed.us/contactus/regions.shtml. The Forest Service site also has interactive maps.

Wrapping Paper, Ribbons, and Greeting Cards

ABUNDANT EARTH

www.abundantearth.com/store/holidaycards.html

The holiday greeting cards sold here are made with 50 percent postconsumer recycled paper and use all-natural vegetable inks.

BLOOMIN' FLOWER CARDS

www.bloomin.com

This site sells biodegradable gift wrap and greeting cards, which are embedded with wildflower seeds and can be planted in the ground or in a pot.

CARE2.COM

www.care2.com

On this site you'll find a wide array of fun, festive e-cards.

CONSERVATREE

www.conservatree.com

Conservatree, a nonprofit dedicated to moving the paper industry more toward recycling, has great information about paper choices.

CREAM CITY RIBBON

www.creamcityribbon.com

This is a good source of natural, biodegradable gift ribbons.

DEWEY HOWARD

www.soapandpaperfactory.com

Here you'll find very cool designer gift wrap—made of recycled paper, of course.

DOLPHIN BLUE

www.dolphinblue.com

This environmentally friendly office-supply store sells a wide assortment of planet-friendly greeting cards.

ECOSOURCE

www.islandnet.com/~ecodette/PAPERSEL.htm

This company sells tree-free paper and envelopes made from 40 percent flax, 40 percent hemp, and 20 percent recovered cotton.

GAIAM

www.gaiam.com

In addition to all kinds of household products and linens, Gaiam sells an impressive assortment of recycled gift bags, wrapping paper (including seed gift wrap, which can be planted), and home decorations, including LED-light reindeer.

GLOBAL HEMP STORE

www.globalhempstore.com

This is a great source of hemp twine.

GREEN FIELD PAPER COMPANY

www.greenfieldpaper.com

This company specializes in tree-free paper products and greeting cards.

THE GREEN OFFICE

www.thegreenoffice.com

This is a complete source for earth-friendly office supplies, including paper products, labels, toner, and furniture.

THE NATURE CONSERVANCY

www.nature.org

The Web site of this conservation groups offers many beautiful nature-inspired e-cards.

NIGHT OWL PAPER GOODS

http://nightowlpapergoods.com

This lovely site sells holiday greeting cards made from recycled wood.

PAP ORGANICS

www.paporganics.com

Not only can you buy gift wrap and stationery made from sustainably grown resources here, you also will find 100 percent natural soy gift ribbon.

PAPERMOJO

www.papermojo.com

PaperMojo is a specialty store with a large selection of papers, including banana fiber paper.

SIERRA CLUB

www.sierraclub.org

The Sierra Club's Web site offers an array of holiday e-cards.

VICKEREY

www.vickerey.com

Vickery is a recycled- and tree-free paper company.

Entertaining

BAMBU

www.bambuhome.com

Here you'll find a range of disposable, biodegradable serving items made of bamboo.

BIOBAGS

www.biobagusa.com

BioBags sells compostable and recyclable kitchen garbage bags, compost-pail liners, and trash bags, all made from corn.

BI-O-KLEEN

www.bi-o-kleen.com

Here you can find ABi-O-Kleen Oxygen Bleach Plus, an alternative to chlorine bleach.

GREEN EARTH, GREEN HOME

www.greenearthgreenhome.com

You'll find more environmentally friendly bleach alternatives and cleaning products here.

PRESERVE

www.recycline.com

Preserve offers a line of recycled plastic plates, kitchenware, and serving ware.

Decorating

BRANCH

www.branchhome.com

A design store whose motto is "sustainable design for living," Branch sells home accessories and green items for pets and children made from sustainable materials in an environmentally friendly manner.

DARTHIA FARM

www.darthiafarm.com

This is the source for beautiful organic wreaths from Maine.

ENVIRO-LOGS

www.enviro-log.net

A green alternative to wood for your fireplace, these "logs" are made from recycled waxed cardboard boxes and produce less smoke than wood logs do.

ENVIRONMENTAL LIGHTS

www.environmentallights.com

Eco-friendly holiday lights are available on this site.

JAVA-LOGS

www.java-log.com

These "logs" are made from coffee grounds; they emit fewer particulates than wood does, and they divert 20 million pounds of coffee waste from landfills every year.

NUBIUS ORGANICS

www.nubiusorganics.com

This site sells a wide variety of stylish and earth-friendly water bottles, travel items, cloth bags, and baby items.

ORGANIC STYLE

www.organicstyle.com

This Web site sells wreaths and garlands as well as green bedding, apparel, food, and pet and bath products.

PETER G CANDLES

www.petergcandles.com

This is a good source of handcrafted all-natural candles.

3R LIVING

www.3rliving.com

This New York–based retailer and Web site sells a full line of eco-friendly products, including books, kitchen items, home decorations, and products for kids and pets.

VIVATERRA

www.vivaterra.com

This is a wonderful Web site for earth-friendly home decor. It's also your source for decorative reindeer made from willow twigs.

Food Items

SUSTAINABLE CAVIAR

Tsar Nicoulai

www.tsarnicoulai.com

This is the place to go for farm-raised caviar from California.

ECOEXPRESS

www.ecoexpress.com

Here you can choose among organic food, gourmet, and bath gift baskets.

FRESH OREGON TRUFFLES

ShireWood Farm

www.shirewoodfarm.com

This organic family farm sells a variety of seasonal fresh truffles.

ORGANIC GIFT BASKETS

www.organicstyle.com

Organic Style (see listing, page 172) also sells holiday baskets filled with organic goodies.

ORGANIC NUTS

Braga Organic Nuts

http://stores.buyorganicnuts.com/StoreFront.bok

A wonderful family-farm source, Braga sells organic pistachios and almonds.

MELISSA'S PRODUCE

www.melissas.com

Organic whole walnuts are available seasonally from this Web site.

ORGANIC PROSCIUTTO

La Quercia

http://laquercia.us

This is an excellent source for artisan cured meats made in Iowa, including prosciutto and pancetta.

Art and Craft Supplies

AFLORAL.COM

www.afloral.com

This floral supplies store carries several types of floral wire.

AMERICAN SPECIALTY GLASS

www.americanspecialtyglass.com

This is a good source of recycled glass chips.

CRAFTER'S PICK

www.crafterspick.com

My favorite brand of tacky glue, Crafter's Pick is available here as well as in art supply stores. Crafter's also makes a line of nontoxic arts and crafts products.

CUFF LINKS.COM

www.cufflinks.com

When you're making your own cuff links, get your cuff link backs here.

ECOWORKS

http://ecoworks.com

This eco-friendly store has a huge supply of nontoxic art supplies called EcoArtWorks, including a full line of recycled paper products, crayons, and pencils.

MAINE WREATH CO.

www.mainewreathco.com

This company sells everything you need to make a wreath, including various types of frames, floral wire, and decorations such as pinecones and ribbon.

STUBBY PENCIL STUDIO

www.stubbypencilstudio.com

This online store sells a wide range of eco-friendly art supplies, including soy crayons, EcoPencils, and recycled sketchbooks.

SWANS CANDLES

http://swanscandles.com/store/CandleWicks.html

This site is a good source of nontoxic pretabbed wicks and other candle-making supplies.

Clothing Recycling Sources

DRESS FOR SUCCESS

www.dressforsuccess.org

A program with locations throughout the United States, Dress for Success donates gently used business attire to disadvantaged women around the world to promote economic independence.

HEART AND SOLE

www.com.msu.edu/pub-rel/heartandsole/index.html

This program, run by Michigan State University's College of Osteopathic Medicine, distributes new and gently used shoes to the needy around the world.

NIKE/LET ME PLAY PROGRAM

www.letmeplay.com/reuseashoe

Nike will accept any brand of sneakers and will recycle them into athletic surfaces.

ONEWARMCOAT.ORG

www.OneWarmCoat.org

Not only is this a source for recycling winter coats, it also has information on how to organize a coat drive.

PATAGONIA COMMON THREADS CLOTHING RECYCLING PROGRAM

www.patagonia.com/usa/patagonia.go?assetid=1956

Patagonia recycles any brand of fleece (and a few other types of sports material) and turns it into new clothing; just mail the clothing in or drop it off at any Patagonia store (only if it's on the way; don't make a special trip).

SOLES UNITED

www.solesunited.com

The Crocs shoe company started the Soles United program, which recycles old Crocs to make new shoes from 20 percent recycled rubber, which it distributes to those in need.

SOLES4SOULS

www.soles4souls.org

This nonprofit also distributes shoes to the needy around the world.

Recycling Sources for Household Items

BATTERIES

To recycle rechargeable batteries, call 1-800-8BATTERY or visit the Rechargeable Battery Recycling Company at www .rbrc.org/call2recycle. If you live in California, you can find detailed information on how to recycle or properly dispose of batteries, which is mandatory under California law, at the Web site of the California Integrated Waste Management Board: www.ciwmb.ca.gov/WPIE/Batteries.

THE BIG GREEN BOX

www.biggreenbox.com

Toxco, a company that handles waste disposal for some local communities, has started a service called the Big Green Box: You order the box, fill it up to 48 pounds with recyclables such as cell phones, batteries, PDA's, laptops, and cameras, and send it back. The fee covers shipping and recycling.

CD RECYCLING CENTER OF AMERICA

www.cdrecyclingcenter.com

Send in your old disks and packaging materials to this recycling center, which accepts all types of CDs and DVDs.

KORKS 4 KIDS

www.korks4kids.com

This is a cork recycling program: You send your corks to them, they use them to make crafts, flooring, and other materials, and the profits are given to children's charities. (Your shipping costs are tax deductible.)

RECORK AMERICA

www.recorkamerica.com

This cork recycling program was created by Amorim, one of the largest Portuguese cork manufacturers.

Acknowledgments

THIS BOOK WAS A TRUE LABOR OF LOVE and would not have been made possible without the joint love, effort, and energy of the below people. I thank you all from the bottom of my heart for your dedication, discipline, vision, and work.

Laura Holmes Hadad, it has been a true pleasure working with you. I will miss our constant contact. Look forward to future collaboration.

Alisa, "solid, solid as a rock."

Shandra, you are truly gifted and such a great friend. The crafts in this book are as much yours as they are mine.

Thank you, Miele, a wonderful Santa's helper.

Thank you to all my eco-experts for your contributions to this book.

Kate Woodrow, Anne Donnard, and the great team at Chronicle Books: thank you for your guidance and commitment to this project.

To my girls in the kitchen, Amy Brown and Mara Abel. You girls rock. And lordy, did we have fun!

Thank you, Ron Hamad, for your never ending upliftment of my creative endeavors. It is always an honor working with you. I know this was a tough one. You are the best.

And thank you so much to his crew including the magical and inventive food stylist Sienna DeGovia; the gifted set designers Kim Pretti and Peggy Wang; super digi-tech Luke Fisher plus Bearded Lady Productions/Ambient Digital, LLC; the awesome Marco Jimenez; Aurelia D'Amore; Chad Hill; Amparo Jelsma; Leah Christiansen; Lindsay Talley; Chris Gordon (a.k.a Sparky); Cory O'Donelle; and Sidney McMullen. I know you all busted your bums, and I appreciate it so much.

And a big thank you to all of the players in the Christmas party photo shoot. You know who you are. That was fun.

Thank you, Greg and India, for putting up with me through it all.

Thank you all who inspire me to do projects like this, that I hope will better our precious planet somehow.

Brenda and Bob Cooke and the Cooke family, how can I thank you enough for allowing us to be in your beautiful space? Thank you, thank you. You are great.

I would also like to thank: Delight Full Inc., Kelly Green Design + Home, and Kelly Van Patten for *so* many of our wonderful eco props, The Hancock Park Homeowners Association, Zenobia Agency, Organic to Go, and Joan's on 3rd.

Index

Table of Equivalents

The exact equivalents in the following tables have been rounded for convenience.

LIQUID/DRY MEASUREMENTS

U.S	METRIC
¼ teaspoon	1.25 milliliters
½ teaspoon	2.5 milliliters
1 teaspoon	5 milliliters
1 tablespoon (3 teaspoons)	15 milliliters
1 fluid ounce (2 tablespoons)	30 milliliters
¼ cup	60 milliliters
⅓ cup	80 milliliters
½ cup	120 milliliters
1 cup	240 milliliters
1 pint (2 cups)	480 milliliters
1 quart (4 cups, 32 ounces)	960 milliliters
1 gallon (4 quarts)	3.84 liters
1 ounce (by weight)	28 grams
1 pound	448 grams
2.2 pounds	1 kilogram

OVEN TEMPERATURE

FAHRENHEIT	CELSIUS	GAS
250	120	½
275	140	1
300	150	2
325	160	3
350	180	4
375	190	5
400	200	6
425	220	7
450	230	8
475	240	9
500	260	10

LENGTHS

U.S.	METRIC
⅛ inch	3 millimeters
¼ inch	6 millimeters
½ inch	12 millimeters
1 inch	2.5 centimeters